MILITARY JUSTICE CASES AND MATERIALS
Second Edition

MILITARY JUSTICE CASES AND MATERIALS

Second Edition

STATUTORY SUPPLEMENT

EUGENE R. FIDELL
Senior Research Scholar in Law and
Florence Rogatz Visiting Lecturer in Law, Yale Law School

ELIZABETH L. HILLMAN
Professor of Law, UC Hastings College of the Law

DWIGHT H. SULLIVAN
Colonel, United States Marine Corps Reserve

ISBN#: 978-1-4224-9988-7

NOTE TO USERS

To ensure that you are using the latest materials available in this area, please be sure to periodically check the LexisNexis Law School web site for downloadable updates and supplements at www.lexisnexis.com/lawschool.

Editorial Offices
121 Chanlon Rd., New Providence, NJ 07974 (908) 464-6800
201 Mission St., San Francisco, CA 94105-1831 (415) 908-3200
www.lexisnexis.com

MATTHEW◆BENDER

TABLE OF CONTENTS

UNIFORM CODE OF MILITARY JUSTICE
10 U.S. Code ch. 47

SUBCHAPTER I.   GENERAL PROVISIONS

§ 801. Art. 1   Definitions

In this chapter.

(1) The term "Judge Advocate General" means, severally, the Judge Advocates General of the Army, Navy, and Air Force and, except when the Coast guard is operating as a service in the Navy, an official designated to serve as Judge Advocate General of the Coast Guard by the Secretary of Homeland Security.

(2) The Navy, the Marine Corps, and the Coast Guard when it is operating as a service in the Navy, shall be considered as one armed force.

(3) The term "commanding officer" includes only commissioned officers.

(4) The term "officer in Charge" means a member of the Navy, the Marine Corps, or the Coast Guard designated as such by appropriate authority.

(5) The term "superior commissioned officer" means a commissioned officer superior in rank or command.

(6) The term "cadet" means a cadet of the United States Military Academy, the United States Air Force Academy, or the United States Coast Guard Academy.

(7) The term "midshipman" means a midshipman of the United States Naval Academy and any other midshipman on active duty in the naval service.

(8) The term "military" refers to any or all of the armed forces.

(9) The term "accuser" means a person who signs and swears to charges, any person who directs that charges nominally be signed and sworn to by another, and any other person who has an interest other than an official interest in the prosecution of the accused.

(10) The term "military judge" means an official of a general or special court-martial detailed in accordance with section 826 of this title (article 26).

(11) The term "law specialist" means a commissioned officer of the Coast Guard designated for special duty (law).

(12) The term "legal officer" means any commissioned officer of the Navy, Marine Corps, or Coast Guard designated to perform legal duties for a command.

(13) The term "judge advocate" means —

(A) an officer of the Judge Advocate General's Corps of the Army or the Navy;

(B) an officer of the Air Force or the Marine Corps who is designated as a judge advocate; or

(C) an officer of the Coast Guard who is designated as a law specialist.

(14) The term "record", when used in connection with the proceedings of a court-martial means —

(A) an official written transcript, written summary, or other writing relating to the proceedings: or

(B) an official audiotape, videotape, or similar material from which sound, or sound and visual images, depicting the proceedings may be reproduced.

(15) The term "classified information" means —

(A) any information or material that has been determined by an official of the United States pursuant to law, an Executive order, or regulation to require protection against unauthorized disclosure for reasons of national security, and

(B) any restricted data, as defined in section 11(y) of the Atomic Energy Act of 1954 (42 U.S.C. 2014(y)).

(16) The term "national security" means the national defense and foreign relations of the United States.

§ 802. Art. 2 Persons subject to this chapter

(a) The following persons are subject to this chapter:

(1) Members of a regular component of the armed forces, including those awaiting discharge after expiration of their terms of enlistment; volunteers from the time of their muster or acceptance into the armed forces; inductees from the time of their actual induction into the armed forces; and other persons lawfully called or ordered into, or to duty in or for training in, the armed forces, from the dates when they are required by the terms of the call or order to obey it.

(2) Cadets, aviation cadets, and midshipmen.

(3) Members of a reserve component while on inactive-duty training, but in

the case of members of the Army National Guard of the United States or the Air National Guard of the United States only when in Federal service.

(4) Retired members of a regular component of the armed forces who are entitled to pay.

(5) Retired members of a reserve component who are receiving hospitalization from an armed force.

(6) Members of the Fleet Reserve and Fleet Marine Corps Reserve.

(7) Persons in custody of the armed forces serving a sentence imposed by a court-martial.

(8) Members of the National Oceanic and Atmospheric Administration, Public Health Service, and other organizations, when assigned to and serving with the armed forces.

(9) Prisoners of war in custody of the armed forces.

(10) In time of declared war or a contingency operation, persons serving with or accompanying an armed force in the field.

(11) Subject to any treaty or agreement to which the United States is or may be a party or to any accepted rule of international law, persons serving with, employed by, or accompanying the armed forces outside the United States and outside the Commonwealth of Puerto Rico, Guam, and the Virgin Islands.

(12) Subject to any treaty or agreement to which the United States is or may be a party or to any accepted rule of international law, persons within an area leased by or otherwise reserved or acquired for the use of the United States which is under the control of the Secretary concerned and which is outside the United States and outside the Commonwealth of Puerto Rico, Guam, and the Virgin Islands.

(13) Individuals belonging to one of the eight categories enumerated in Article 4 of the Convention Relative to the Treatment of Prisoners of War, done at Geneva August 12, 1949 (6 UST 3316), who violate the law of war.

(b) The voluntary enlistment of any person who has the capacity to understand the significance of enlisting in the armed forces shall be valid for purposes of jurisdiction under subsection (a) and a change of status from civilian to member of the armed forces shall be effective upon the taking of the oath of enlistment.

(c) Notwithstanding any other provision of law, a person serving with an armed force who —

(1) submitted voluntarily to military authority;

(2) met the mental competence and minimum age qualifications of sections 504 and 505 of this title at the time of voluntary submissions to military authority:

(3) received military pay or allowances; and

(4) performed military duties;

is subject to this chapter until such person's active service has been terminated in accordance with law or regulations promulgated by the Secretary concerned.

(d) (1) A member of a reserve component who is not on active duty and who is made the subject of proceedings under section 815 (article 15) or section 830 (article 30) with respect to an offense against this chapter may be ordered to active duty involuntary for the purpose of

(A) investigation under section 832 of this title (article 32);

(B) trial by court-martial; or

(C) nonjudicial punishment under section 815 of this title (article15).

(2) A member of a reserve component may not be ordered to active duty under paragraph (1) except with respect to an offense committed while the member was

(A) on active duty; or

(B) on inactive-duty training, but in the case of members of the Army National Guard of the United States or the Air National Guard of the United States only when in Federal service.

(3) Authority to order a member to active duty under paragraph (1) shall be exercised under regulations prescribed by the President.

(4) A member may be ordered to active duty under paragraph (1) only by a person empowered to convene general courts-martial in a regular component of the armed forces.

(5) A member ordered to active duty under paragraph (1), unless the order to active duty was approved by the Secretary concerned, may not

(A) be sentenced to confinement; or

(B) be required to serve a punishment consisting of any restriction on liberty during a period other than a period of inactive-duty training or active duty (other than active duty ordered under paragraph (1)).

(e) The provisions of this section are subject to section 876(d)(2) of this title (article 76b(d)(2).

§ 803. Art. 3 Jurisdiction to try certain personnel

(a) Subject to section 843 of this title (article 43), no person who is in a status in which the person is subject to this chapter and who committed an offense against this chapter while formerly in a status in which the person was subject to this chapter is not relieved from amenability to the jurisdiction of this chapter for that offense by reason of a termination of that person's former status.

(b) Each person discharged from the armed forces who is later charged with having fraudulently obtained his discharge is, subject to section 843 of this title (article 43), subject to trial by court-martial on that charge and is after apprehension subject to trial by court-martial on that charge and is after apprehension subject to this chapter while in the custody of the armed forces for that trial. Upon conviction of that charge he is subject to trial by court-martial for all offenses under this chapter committed before the fraudulent discharge.

(c) No person who has deserted from the armed forces may be relieved from amenability to the jurisdiction of this chapter by virtue of separation from any later period of service.

(d) A member of a reserve component who is subject to this chapter is not, by virtue of the termination of a period of active duty or inactive-duty training, relieved from amenability to the jurisdiction of this chapter for an offense against this chapter committed during such period of active duty or inactive-duty training.

§ 804. Art. 4   Dismissed officer's right to trial by court-martial

(a) If any commissioned officer, dismissed by order of the President, makes a written application for trial by court-martial setting forth, under oath, that he has been wrongfully dismissed, the President, as soon as practicable, shall convene a general court-martial to try that officer on the charges on which he was dismissed. A court-martial so convened has jurisdiction to try the dismissed officer on those charges, and he shall be considered to have waived the right to plead any statute of limitations applicable to any offense with which he is charged. The court-martial may, as part of its sentence, adjudge the affirmance of the dismissal, but if the court-martial acquits the accused or if the sentence adjudged, as finally approved or affirmed, does not include dismissal or death, the Secretary concerned shall substitute for the dismissal ordered by the President a form of discharge authorized for administrative issue.

(b) If the President fails to convene a general court-martial within six months from the preparation of an application for trial under this article, the Secretary concerned shall substitute for the dismissal order by the President a form of discharge authorized for administrative issue.

(c) If a discharge is substituted for a dismissal under this article, the President alone may reappoint the officer to such commissioned grade and with such rank as, in the opinion of the President, that former officer would have attained had he not been dismissed. The reappointment of such a former officer shall be without regard to the existence of a vacancy and shall affect the promotion status of other officers only insofar as the President may direct. All time between the dismissal and the reappointment shall be considered as actual service for all purposes, including the right to pay and allowances.

(d) If an officer is discharged from any armed force by administrative action or is dropped from the rolls by order of the President, he has no right to trial under this article.

§ 805. Art. 5   Territorial Applicability of this chapter

This chapter applies in all places.

§ 806. Art. 6   Judge Advocates and legal officers

(a) The assignment for duty of judge advocates of the Army, Navy, Air Force, and Coast Guard shall be made upon the recommendation of the Judge Advocate General of the armed force of which they are members. The assignment for duty of judge advocate of the Marine Corps shall be made by direction of the Commandant of the Marine Corps. The Judge Advocate General or senior members of his staff shall make frequent inspection in the field in supervision of the administration of military justice.

(b) Convening authorities shall at all times communicate directly with their staff judge advocates or legal officers in matters relating to the administration of military justice; and the staff judge advocate or legal officer of any command is entitled to communicate directly with the staff judge advocate or legal officer of a superior or subordinate command, or with the Judge Advocate General.

(c) No person who has acted as member, military judge, trial counsel, assistant trial counsel, defense counsel, assistant defense counsel, or investigating officer in any case may later act as a staff judge advocate or legal officer to any reviewing authority upon the same case.

(d) (1) A judge advocate who is assigned or detailed to perform the functions of a civil office in the Government of the United States under section 973(b)(2)(B) of this title may perform such duties as may be requested by the agency concerned, including representation of the United States in civil and criminal cases.

(2) The Secretary of Defense, and the Secretary of Homeland Security with respect to the Coast Guard when it in not operating as a service in the Navy, shall prescribe regulations providing that reimbursement may be a condition of assistance by judge advocates assigned or detailed under section 973(b)(2)(B) of this title.

§ 806a. Art. 6a   Investigation and disposition of matters pertaining to the fitness of military judges

(a) The President shall prescribe procedures for the investigation and disposition of charges, allegations, or information pertaining to the fitness of a military judge or military appellate judge to perform the duties of the judge's position. To the extent practicable, the procedures shall be uniform for all armed forces.

(b) The President shall transmit a copy of the procedures prescribed pursuant to this section to the Committees on Armed Services of the Senate and the House of Representatives.

SUBCHAPTER II.   APPREHENSION AND RESTRAINT

§ 807. Art. 7   Apprehension

(a) Apprehension is the taking of a person into custody.

(b) Any person authorized under regulations governing the armed forces to apprehend persons subject to this chapter or to trial thereunder may do so upon reasonable belief that an offense has been committed and that the person apprehended committed it.

(c) Commissioned officers, warrant officers, petty officers, and noncommissioned officers have authority to quell quarrels, frays and disorders among persons subject to this chapter who take part therein.

§ 808. Art. 8   Apprehension of deserters

Any civil officer having authority to apprehend offenders under the laws of the United States or of a State, Territory, Commonwealth, or possession, or the District of Columbia may summarily apprehend a deserter from the armed forces and deliver him into the custody of those forces.

§ 809. Art. 9   Imposition of restraint

(a) Arrest is the restraint of a person by an order, not imposed as a punishment for an offense, directing him to remain within certain specified limits. Confinement is the physical restraint of a person.

(b) An enlisted member may be ordered into arrest or confinement by any commissioned officer by an order, oral or written, delivered in person or through other persons subject to this chapter. A commanding officer may authorize warrant officers, petty officers, or noncommissioned officers to order enlisted members of his command or subject to his authority into arrest or confinement.

(c) A commissioned officer, a warrant officer, or a civilian subject to this chapter or to trial thereunder may be ordered into arrest or confinement only by a commanding officer to whose authority he is subject, by an order, oral or written, delivered in person or by another commissioned officer. The authority to order such persons into arrest or confinement may not be delegated.

(d) No person may be ordered into arrest or confinement except for probable cause.

(e) Nothing in this article limits the authority of persons authorized to apprehend offenders to secure the custody of an alleged offender until proper authority may be notified.

§ 810. Art. 10   Restraint of persons charged with offenses

Any person subject to this chapter charged with an offense under this chapter shall be ordered into arrest or confinement, as circumstances may require; but when charged only with an offense normally tried by a summary court-martial, he shall not ordinarily be placed in confinement. When any person subject to this chapter is placed in arrest or confinement prior to trial, immediate steps shall be taken to inform him of the specific wrong of which he is accused and to try him or to dismiss the charges and release him.

§ 811. Art. 11   Reports and receiving of prisoners

(a) No provost marshal, commander or a guard, or master at arms may refuse to receive or keep any prisoner committed to his charge by a commissioned officer of the armed forces, when the committing officer furnishes a statement, signed by him, of the offense charged against the prisoner.

(b) Every commander of a guard or master at arms to whose charge a prisoner is committed shall, within twenty-four hours after that commitment or as soon as he is relieved from guard, report to the commanding officer the name of the prisoner, the offense charged against him, and the name of the person who ordered or authorized the commitment.

§ 812. Art. 12 Confinement with enemy prisoners prohibited

No member of the armed forces may be placed in confinement in immediate association with enemy prisoners or other foreign nationals not members of the armed forces.

§ 813. Art. 13 Punishment prohibited before trial

No person, while being held for trial, may be subjected to punishment or penalty other than arrest or confinement upon the charges pending against him, nor shall the arrest or confinement imposed upon him be any more rigorous than the circumstances required to insure his presence, but he may be subjected to minor punishment during that period for infractions of discipline.

§ 814. Art. 14 Delivery of offenders to civil authorities

(a) Under such regulations as the Secretary concerned may prescribe, a member of the armed forces accused of an offense against civil authority may be delivered, upon request, to the civil authority for trial.

(b) When delivery under this article is made to any civil authority of a person undergoing sentence of a court-martial, the delivery, if followed by conviction in a civil tribunal, interrupts the execution of the sentence of the court-martial, and the offender after having answered to the civil authorities for his offense shall, upon the request of competent military authority, be returned to military custody for the completion of his sentence.

SUBCHAPTER III. NON-JUDICIAL PUNISHMENT

§ 815. Art. 15 Commanding officer's non-judicial punishment

(a) Under such regulations as the President may prescribe, and under such additional regulations as may be prescribed by the Secretary concerned, limitations may be placed on the powers granted by this article with respect to the kind and amount of punishment authorized, the categories of commanding officers and warrant officers exercising command authorized to exercise those powers, the applicability of this article to an accused who demands trial by court-martial, and the kinds of courts-martial to which the case may be referred upon such a demand. However, except in the case of a member attached to or embarked in a vessel, punishment may not be imposed upon any member of the armed forces under this article if the member has, before the imposition of such punishment, demanded trial by court-martial in lieu of such punishment. Under similar regulations, rules may be prescribed with respect to the suspension of punishments authorized hereunder. If authorized by regulations of the Secretary concerned, a commanding officer exercising general court-martial jurisdiction or an officer of general or flag rank in command may delegate his powers under this article to a principal assistant.

(b) Subject to subsection (a) any commanding officer may, in addition to or in lieu of admonition or reprimand, impose one or more of the following disciplinary punishments for minor offenses without the intervention of a court-martial —

(1) upon officers of his command —

(A) restriction to certain specified limits, with or without suspension from duty, for not more that 30 consecutive days;

(B) if imposed by an officer exercising general court-martial jurisdictions or an officer of general flag rank in command

(i) arrest in quarters for not more than 30 consecutive days;

(ii) forfeiture of not more than one-half of one month's pay per month for two months;

(iii) restriction to certain specified limits, with or without suspension from duty, for not more than 60 consecutive days;

(iv) detention of not more than one-half of one month's pay per month for three months;

(2) upon other personnel of his command —

(A) if imposed upon a person attached to or embarked in a vessel, confinement on bread and water or diminished rations for not more than three consecutive days;

(B) correctional custody for not more than seven consecutive days;

(C) forfeiture of not more than seven days' pay;

(D) reduction to the next inferior pay grade, if the grade from which demoted is within the promotion authority of the officer imposing the reduction or any officer subordinate to the one who imposes the reduction;

(E) extra duties, including fatigue or other duties, for not more than 14 consecutive days;

(F) restriction to certain specified limits, with or without suspension from duty, for not more than 14 consecutive days;

(G) detention of not more than 14 days' pay;

(H) if imposed by an officer of the grade of major or lieutenant commander, or above

(i) the punishment authorized under clause (A);

(ii) correctional custody for not more than 30 consecutive days;

(iii) forfeiture of not more than one-half of one month's pay per month for two months;

(iv) reduction to the lowest or any intermediate pay grade, if the grade from which demoted is within the promotion authority of the officer imposing the reduction or any officer subordinate to the one who imposes the reduction, but an enlisted member in a pay grade above E-4 may not be reduced more than two pay grades;

(v) extra duties, including fatigue or other duties, for not more than 45 consecutive days;

(vi) restriction to certain specified limits, with or without suspension from duty, for not more than 60 consecutive days;

(vii) detention of not more than one-half of one month's pay per month for three months.

Detention of pay shall be for a stated period of not more than one year but if the offender's term of service expires earlier, the detention shall terminate upon that expiration. No two or more of the punishments of arrest in quarters, confinement or bread and water or diminished rations, correctional custody, extra duties, and restriction may be combined to run consecutively in the maximum amount imposable for each. Whenever any of those punishments are combined to run consecutively, there must be an apportionment. In addition, forfeiture of pay may not be combined with detention of pay without an apportionment. For the purpose of this subsection, "correctional custody" is the physical restraint of a person during duty or nonduty hours and may include extra duties, fatigue duties, or hard labor. If practicable, correctional custody will not be served in immediate association with persons awaiting trial or held in confinement pursuant to trial by court-martial.

(c) An officer in charge may impose upon enlisted members assigned to the unit of which he is in charge such of the punishment authorized under subsection (b)(2)(A)-(G) as the Secretary concerned may specifically prescribe by regulation.

(d) The officer who imposes the punishment authorized in subsection (b), or his successor in command, may, at any time, suspend probationally any part or amount of the unexecuted punishment imposed and may suspend probationally a reduction in grade or forfeiture imposed under subsection (b), whether or not executed. In addition, he may, at any time, remit or mitigate any part or amount of the unexecuted punishment imposed and may set aside in whole or in part the punishment, whether executed or unexecuted, and restore all rights, privileges and property affected. He may also mitigate reduction in grade to forfeiture or detention of pay. When mitigating —

(1) arrest in quarters to restriction;

(2) confinement on bread and water or diminished rations to correctional custody;

(3) correctional custody or confinement on bread and water or diminished rations to extra duties or restriction, or both; or

(4) extra duties to restriction; the mitigated punishment shall not be for a greater period than the punishment mitigated. When mitigating forfeiture of pay to detention of pay, the amount of detention shall not be greater than the amount of the forfeiture. When mitigating reduction in grade to forfeiture or detention of pay, the amount of the forfeiture or detention shall not be greater

than the amount that could have been imposed initially under this article by the officer who imposed the punishment mitigated.

(e) A person punished under this article who considers his punishment unjust or disproportionate to the offense may, through proper channels, appeal to the next superior authority. The appeal shall be promptly forwarded and decided, but the person punished may in the meantime be required to undergo the punishment adjudged. The superior authority may exercise the same powers with respect to the punishment imposed as may be exercised under subsection (d) by the officer who imposed the punishment. Before acting on appeal from a punishment of —

(1) arrest in quarters for more than seven days;

(2) correctional custody for more than seven days;

(3) forfeiture of more than seven days' pay;

(4) reduction of one or more pay grades from the fourth or a higher pay grade;

(5) extra duties for more than 14 days;

(6) restriction for more than 14 days; or

(7) detention of more than 14 days' pay;

the authority who is to act on the appeal shall refer the case to a judge advocate or a lawyer of the Department of Homeland Security for consideration and advice, and may so refer the case upon appeal from any punishment imposed under subsection (b).

(f) The imposition and enforcement of disciplinary punishment under this article for any act or omission is not a bar to trial by court-martial for a serious crime or offense growing out of the same act or omission, and not properly punishable under this article; but the fact that a disciplinary punishment has been enforced may be shown by the accused upon trial, and when so shown shall be considered in determining the measure of punishment to be adjudged in the event of a finding of guilty.

(g) The Secretary concerned may, by regulation, prescribe the form of records to be kept under this article and may also prescribe that certain categories of those proceedings shall be in writing.

SUBCHAPTER IV.   COURT-MARTIAL JURISDICTION

§ 816. Art. 16   Courts-martial classified

The three kinds of courts-martial in each of the armed forces are —

(1) general courts-martial, consisting of —

(A) a military judge and not less than five members or, in a case in which the accused may be sentenced to a penalty of death, the number of members determined under section 825a of this title (article 25a); or

(B) only a military judge, if before the court is assembled the accused, knowing the identity of the military judge and after consultation with defense counsel, requests orally on the record or in writing a court composed only of a military judge and the military judge approves;

(2) special courts-martial, consisting of —

(A) not less than three members; or

(B) a military judge and not less than three members; or

(C) only a military judge, if one has been detailed to the court, and the accused under the same conditions as those prescribed in clause (1)(B) so requests; and

(3) summary courts-martial, consisting of one commissioned officer.

§ 817. Art. 17   Jurisdiction of courts-martial in general

(a) Each armed force has court-martial jurisdiction over all persons subject to this chapter. The exercise of jurisdiction by one armed force over personnel of another armed force shall be in accordance with regulations prescribed by the President.

(b) In all cases, departmental review after that by the officer with authority to convene a general court-martial for the command which held the trial, where that review is required under this chapter, shall be carried out by the department that includes the armed force of which the accused is a member.

§ 818. Art. 18   Jurisdiction of general courts-martial

Subject to section 817 of this title (article 17), general courts-martial have jurisdiction to try persons subject to this chapter for any offense made punishable by this chapter and may, under such limitations as the President may prescribe, adjudge any punishment not forbidden by this chapter, including the penalty of death when specifically authorized by this chapter. General courts-martial also have jurisdiction to try any person who by the law of war is subject to trial by a military tribunal and may adjudge any punishment permitted by the law of war. However, a general court-martial of the kind specified in section 816(1)(B) of this title (article 16(1)(B)) shall not have jurisdiction to try any person for any offense for which the death penalty may be adjudged unless the case has been previously referred to trial as a noncapital case.

§ 819. Art. 19   Jurisdiction of special courts-martial

Subject to section 817 of this title (article 17), special courts-martial have jurisdiction to try persons subject to this chapter for any noncapital offense made punishable by this chapter and, under such regulations as the President may prescribe, for capital offenses. Special courts-martial may, under such limitations as the President may prescribe, adjudge any punishment not forbidden by this chapter except death, dishonorable discharge, dismissal, confinement for more than one year, hard labor without confinement for more than three months, forfeiture of pay exceeding two-thirds pay per month, or forfeiture of pay for more than one year. A bad-conduct discharge, confinement for more than six months, or forfeiture of pay for more than six months may not be adjudged unless a complete record of the proceedings and testimony has been made, counsel having the qualifications prescribed under section 827(b) of this title (article 27(b)) was detailed to represent the accused, and a military judge was detailed to the trial, except in any case in which a military judge could not be detailed to the trial because of physical conditions or military exigencies. In any such case in which a military judge was not detailed to the trial, the convening authority shall make a detailed written statement, to be appended to the record, stating the reason or reasons a military judge could not be detailed.

§ 820. Art. 20   Jurisdiction of summary courts-martial

Subject to section 817 of this title (article 17), summary courts-martial have jurisdiction to try persons subject to this chapter, except officers, cadets, aviation cadets, and midshipmen, for any noncapital offense made punishable by this chapter. No person with respect to whom summary courts-martial have jurisdiction may be brought to trial before a summary court-martial if he objects thereto. If objection to trial by summary court-martial is made by an accused, trial shall be ordered by special or general court-martial, as may be appropriate. Summary courts-martial may, under such limitations as the President may prescribe, adjudge any punishment not forbidden by this chapter except death, dismissal, dishonorable or bad-conduct discharge, confinement for more than one month, hard-labor without confinement for more than 45 days, restriction to specified limits for more than two months, or forfeiture of more than two-thirds of one month's pay.

§ 821. Art. 21   Jurisdiction of courts-martial not exclusive

The provisions of this chapter conferring jurisdiction upon courts-martial do not deprive military commissions, provost courts, or other military tribunals of concurrent jurisdiction with respect to offenders or offenses that by statute or by the law of war may be tried by military commissions, provost courts, or other military tribunals. This section does not apply to a military commission established under chapter 47A of this title.

SUBCHAPTER V.   COMPOSITION OF COURTS-MARTIAL

§ 822. Art. 22   Who may convene general courts-martial

(a) General courts-martial may be convened by —

(1) the President of the United States;

(2) the Secretary of Defense;

(3) the commanding officer of a unified or specified combatant command;

(4) the Secretary concerned;

(5) the commanding officer of an Army Group, an Army, an Army Corps, a division, a separate brigade, or a corresponding unit of the Army or Marine Corps;

(6) the commander in chief of a fleet; the commanding officer of a naval

station or larger shore activity of the Navy beyond the United States;

(7) the commanding officer of an air command, an air force, an air division, or a separate wing of the Air Force or Marine Corps;

(8) any other commanding officer designated by the Secretary concerned; or

(9) any other commanding officer in any of the armed forces when empowered by the President.

(b) If any such commanding officer is an accuser, the court shall be convened by superior competent authority, and may in any case be convened by such authority if considered desirable by him.

§ 823. Art. 23   Who may convene special courts-martial

(a) Special courts-martial may be convened by —

(1) any person who may convene a general court-martial;

(2) the commanding officer of a district, garrison, fort, camp, station, Air Force base, auxiliary air field, or other place where members of the Army or the Air Force are on duty;

(3) the commanding officer of a brigade, regiment, detached battalion, or corresponding unit of the Army;

(4) the commanding officer of a wing, group, or separate squadron of the Air Force;

(5) the commanding officer of any naval or Coast Guard vessel, shipyard, base, or station; the commanding officer of any Marine brigade, regiment, detached battalion, or corresponding unit; the commanding officer of any Marine barracks, wing, group, separate squadron, station, base, auxiliary air field, or other place where members of the Marine Corps are on duty;

(6) the commanding officer of any separate or detached command or group of detached units of any of the armed forces placed under a single commander for this purpose; or

(7) the commanding officer or officer in charge of any other command when empowered by the Secretary concerned.

(b) If any such officer is an accuser, the court shall be convened by superior competent authority, and may in any case be convened by such authority if considered advisable by him.

§ 824. Art. 24   Who may convene summary courts-martial

(a) Summary courts-martial may be convened by —

(1) any person who may convene a general or special court-martial;

(2) the commanding officer of a detached company, or other detachment of the Army;

(3) the commanding officer of a detached squadron or other detachment of

the Air Force; or

(4) the commanding officer or officer in charge of any other command when empowered by the Secretary concerned.

(b) When only one commissioned officer is present with a command or detachment he shall be the summary court-martial of that command or detachment and shall hear and determine all summary court-martial cases brought before him. Summary courts-martial may, however, be convened in any case by superior competent authority when considered desirable by him.

§ 825. Art. 25 Who may serve on courts-martial

(a) Any commissioned officer on active duty is eligible to serve on all courts-martial for the trial of any person who may lawfully be brought before such courts for trial.

(b) Any warrant officer on active duty is eligible to serve on general and special courts-martial for the trial of any person, other than a commissioned officer, who may lawfully be brought before such courts for trial.

(c) (1) Any enlisted member of an armed force on active duty who is not a member of the same unit as the accused is eligible to serve on general and special courts-martial for the trial of any enlisted member of an armed force who may lawfully be brought before such courts for trial, but he shall serve as a member of a court only if, before the conclusion of a session called by the military judge under section 839(a) of this title (article 39(a)) prior to trial or, in the absence of such a session, before the court is assembled for the trial of the accused, the accused personally has requested orally on the record or in writing that enlisted members serve on it. After such a request, the accused may not be tried by a general or special court-martial the membership of which does not include enlisted members in a number comprising at least one-third of the total membership of the court, unless eligible enlisted members cannot be obtained on account of physical conditions or military exigencies. If such members cannot be obtained, the court may be assembled and the trial held without them, but the convening authority shall make a detailed written statement, to be appended to the record, stating why they could not be obtained.

(2) In this article, "unit" means any regularly organized body as defined by the Secretary concerned, but in no case may it be a body larger than a company, squadron, ship's crew, or body corresponding to one of them.

(d) (1) When it can be avoided, no member of an armed force may be tried by a court-martial any member of which is junior to him in rank or grade.

(2) When convening a court-martial, the convening authority shall detail as members thereof such members of the armed forces as, in his opinion, are best qualified for the duty by reason of age, education, training, experience, length of service, and judicial temperament. No member of an armed force is eligible to serve as a member of a general or special court-martial when he is the accuser or a witness for the prosecution or has acted as investigating officer or

as counsel in the same case.

(e) Before a court-martial is assembled for the trial of a case, the convening authority may excuse a member of the court from participating in the case. Under such regulations as the Secretary concerned may prescribe, the convening authority may delegate his authority under this subsection to his staff judge advocate or legal officer or to any other principal assistant.

§ 825a. Art. 25a   Number of members in capital cases

In a case in which the accused may be sentenced to a penalty of death, the number of members shall be not less than 12, unless 12 members are not reasonably available because of physical conditions or military exigencies, in which case the convening authority shall specify a lesser number of members not less than five, and the court may be assembled and the trial held with not less than the number of members so specified. In such a case, the convening authority shall make a detailed written statement, to be appended to the record, stating why a greater number of members were not reasonably available.

§ 826. Art. 26   Military judge of a general or special court-martial

(a) A military judge shall be detailed to each general court-martial. Subject to regulations of the Secretary concerned, a military judge may be detailed to any special court-martial. The Secretary concerned shall prescribe regulations providing for the manner in which military judges are detailed for such courts-martial and for the persons who are authorized to detail military judges for such courts-martial. The military judge shall preside over each open session of the court-martial to which he has been detailed.

(b) A military judge shall be a commissioned officer of the armed forces who is a member of the bar of a Federal court or a member of the bar of the highest court of a State and who is certified to be qualified for duty as a military judge by the Judge Advocate General of the armed force of which such military judge is a member.

(c) The military judge of a general court-martial shall be designated by the Judge Advocate General, or his designee, of the armed force of which the military judge is a member for detail in accordance with regulations prescribed under subsection (a). Unless the court-martial was convened by the President or the Secretary concerned, neither the convening authority nor any member of his staff shall prepare or review any report concerning the effectiveness, fitness, or efficiency of the military judge so detailed, which relates to his performance of duty as a military judge. A commissioned officer who is certified to be qualified for duty as a military judge of a general court-martial may perform such duties only when he is assigned and directly responsible to the Judge Advocate General, or his designee, of the armed force of which the military judge is a member and may perform duties of a judicial or nonjudicial nature other than those relating to his primary duty as a military judge of a general court-martial when such duties are assigned to him by or with the approval of that Judge Advocate General or his designee.

(d) No person is eligible to act as military judge in a case if he is the accuser or a witness for the prosecution or has acted as investigating officer or a counsel in the same case.

(e) The military judge of a court-martial may not consult with the members of the court except in the presence of the accused, trial counsel, and defense counsel, nor may he vote with the members of the court.

§ 827. Art. 27   Detail of trial counsel and defense counsel

(a) (1) Trial counsel and defense counsel shall be detailed for each general and special court-martial. Assistant trial counsel and assistant and associate defense counsel may be detailed for each general and special court-martial. The Secretary concerned shall prescribe regulations providing for the manner in which counsel are detailed for such courts-martial and for the persons who are authorized to detail counsel for such courts-martial.

(2) No person who has acted as investigating officer, military judge, or court member in any case may act later as trial counsel, assistant trial counsel, or, unless expressly requested by the accused, as defense counsel or assistant or associate defense counsel in the same case. No person who has acted for the prosecution may act later in the same case for the defense, nor may any person who has acted for the defense act later in the same case for the prosecution.

(b) Trial counsel or defense counsel detailed for a general court-martial —

(1) must be a judge advocate who is a graduate of an accredited law school or is a member of the bar of a Federal court or of the highest court of a State; or must be a member of the bar of a Federal court or of the highest court of a State; and

(2) must be certified as competent to perform such duties by the Judge Advocate General of the armed force of which he is a member.

(c) In the case of a special court-martial —

(1) the accused shall be afforded the opportunity to be represented at the trial by counsel having the qualifications prescribed under section 827(b) of this title (article 27(b)) unless counsel having such qualifications cannot be obtained on account of physical conditions or military exigencies. If counsel having such qualifications cannot be obtained, the court may be convened and the trial held but the convening authority shall make a detailed written statement, to be appended to the record, stating why counsel with such qualifications could not be obtained;

(2) if the trial counsel is qualified to act as counsel before a general court-martial, the defense counsel detailed by the convening authority must be a person similarly qualified; and

(3) if the trial counsel is a judge advocate or a member of the bar of a Federal court or the highest court of a State, the defense counsel detailed by the convening authority must be one of the foregoing.

§ 828. Art. 28   Detail or employment of reporters and interpreters

Under such regulations as the Secretary concerned may prescribe, the convening authority of a court-martial, military commission, or court of inquiry shall detail or employ qualified court reporters, who shall record the proceedings of and testimony taken before that court or commission. Under like regulations the convening authority of a court-martial, military commission, or court of inquiry may detail or employ interpreters who shall interpret for the court or commission. This section does not apply to a military commission established under chapter 47A of this title.

§ 829. Art. 29　Absent and additional members

(a) No member of a general or special court-martial may be absent or excused after the court has been assembled for the trial of the accused unless excused as a result of a challenge, excused by the military judge for physical disability or other good cause, or excused by order of the convening authority for good cause.

(b) (1) Whenever a general court-martial, other than a general court-martial composed of a military judge only, is reduced below the applicable minimum number of members, the trial may not proceed unless the convening authority details new members sufficient in number to provide not less than the applicable minimum number of members. The trial may proceed with the new members present after the recorded evidence previously introduced before the members of the court has been read to the court in the presence of the military judge, the accused, and counsel for both sides.

(2) In this section, the term "applicable minimum number of members" means five members or, in a case in which the death penalty may be adjudged, the number of members determined under section 825a of this title (article 25a).

(c) Whenever a special court-martial, other than a special court-martial composed of a military judge only, is reduced below three members, the trial may not proceed unless the convening authority details new members sufficient in number to provide not less than three members. The trial shall proceed with the new members present as if no evidence had previously been introduced at the trial, unless a verbatim record of the evidence previously introduced before the members of the court or a stipulation thereof is read to the court in the presence of the military judge, if any, the accused and counsel for both sides.

(d) If the military judge of a court-martial composed of a military judge only is unable to proceed with the trial because of physical disability, as a result of a challenge, or for other good cause, the trial shall proceed, subject to any applicable conditions of section 816(1)(B) or (2)(C) of this title (article 16(1)(B) or (2)(C)), after the detail of a new military judge as if no evidence had previously been introduced, unless a verbatim record of the evidence previously introduced or a stipulation thereof is read in court in the presence of the new military judge, the accused, and counsel for both sides.

SUBCHAPTER VI.   PRE-TRIAL PROCEDURE

§ 830. Art. 30   Charges and specifications

(a) Charges and specifications shall be signed by a person subject to this chapter under oath before a commissioned officer of the armed forces authorized to administer oaths and shall state —

(1) that the signer has personal knowledge of, or has investigated, the matters set forth therein; and

(2) that they are true in fact to the best of his knowledge and belief.

(b) Upon the preferring of charges, the proper authority shall take immediate steps to determine what disposition should be made thereof in the interest of justice and discipline, and the person accused shall be informed of the charges against him as soon as practicable.

§ 831. Art. 31   Compulsory self-incrimination prohibited

(a) No person subject to this chapter may compel any person to incriminate himself or to answer any question the answer to which may tend to incriminate him.

(b) No person subject to this chapter may interrogate, or request any statement from, an accused or a person suspected of an offense without first informing him of the nature of the accusation and advising him that he does not have to make any statement regarding the offense of which he is accused or suspected and that any statement made by him may be used as evidence against him in a trial by court-martial.

(c) No person subject to this chapter may compel any person to make a statement or produce evidence before any military tribunal if the statement or evidence is not material to the issue and may tend to degrade him.

(d) No statement obtained from any person in violation of this article, or through the use of coercion, unlawful influence, or unlawful inducement may be received in evidence against him in a trial by court-martial.

§ 832. Art. 32   Investigation

(a) No charge or specification may be referred to a general court-martial for trial until a thorough and impartial investigation of all the matters set forth therein has been made. This investigation shall include inquiry as to the truth of the matter set forth in the charges, consideration of the form of charges, and a recommendation as to the disposition which should be made of the case in the interest of justice and discipline.

(b) The accused shall be advised of the charges against him and of his right to be represented at that investigation by counsel. The accused has the right to be represented at that investigation as provided in section 838 of this title (article 38) and in regulations prescribed under that section. At that investigation full opportunity shall be given to the accused to cross-examine witnesses against him if they are available and to present anything he may desire in his own behalf, either in defense or mitigation, and the investigating officer shall examine available witnesses requested by the accused. If the charges are forwarded after the investigation, they shall be accompanied by a statement of the substance of the testimony taken on both sides and a copy thereof shall be given to the accused.

(c) If an investigation of the subject matter of an offense has been conducted before the accused is charged with the offense, and if the accused was present at the investigation and afforded the opportunities for representation, cross-examination, and presentation prescribed in subsection (b), no further investigation of that charge is necessary under this article unless it is demanded by the accused after he is informed of the charge. A demand for further investigation entitles the accused to recall witnesses for further cross-examination and to offer any new evidence in his own behalf.

(d) If evidence adduced in an investigation under this article indicates that the accused committed an uncharged offense, the investigating officer may investigate the subject matter of that offense without the accused having first been charged with the offense if the accused —

(1) is present at the investigation;

(2) is informed of the nature of each uncharged offense investigated; and

(3) is afforded the opportunities for representation, cross-examination, and presentation prescribed in subsection (b).

(e) The requirements of this article are binding on all persons administering this chapter but failure to follow them does not constitute jurisdictional error.

§ 833. Art. 33   Forwarding of charges

When a person is held for trial by general court-martial the commanding officer shall, within eight days after the accused is ordered into arrest or confinement, if practicable, forward the charges, together with the investigation and allied papers, to the officer exercising general court-martial jurisdiction. If that is not practicable, he shall report in writing to that officer the reasons for delay.

§ 834. Art. 34   Advice of staff judge advocate and reference for trial

(a) Before directing the trial of any charge by general court-martial, the convening authority shall refer it to his staff judge advocate for consideration and advice. The convening authority may not refer a specification under a charge to a general court-martial for trial unless he has been advised in writing by the staff judge advocate that —

(1) the specification alleges an offense under this chapter;

(2) the specification is warranted by the evidence indicated in the report of investigation under section 832 of this title (article 32)(if there is such a report); and

(3) a court-martial would have jurisdiction over the accused and the offense.

(b) The advice of the staff judge advocate under subsection (a) with respect to a specification under a charge shall include a written and signed statement by the staff judge advocate —

(1) expressing his conclusions with respect to each matter set forth in subsection (a); and

(2) recommending action that the convening authority take regarding the specification.

If the specification is referred for trial, the recommendation of the staff judge advocate shall accompany the specification.

(c) If the charges or specifications are not formally correct or do not conform to the substance of the evidence contained in the report of the investigating officer, formal corrections, and such changes in the charges and specifications as are needed to make them conform to the evidence, may be made.

§ 835. Art. 35   Service of charges

The trial counsel to whom court-martial charges are referred for trial shall cause to be served upon the accused a copy of the charges upon which trial is to be had. In time of peace no person may, against his objection, be brought to trial, or be required to participate by himself or counsel in a session called by the military judge under section 839(a) of this title (article 39(a)), in a general court-martial case within a period of five days after the service of charges upon him, or in a special court-martial case within a period of three days after the service of charges upon him.

SUBCHAPTER VII.   TRIAL PROCEDURE

§ 836. Art. 36   President may prescribe rules

(a) Pretrial, trial, and post-trial procedures, including modes of proof, for cases arising under this chapter triable in courts-martial, military commissions and other military tribunals, and procedures for courts of inquiry, may be prescribed by the President by regulations which shall, so far as he considers practicable, apply the principles of law and the rules of evidence generally recognized in the trial of criminal cases in the United States district courts, but which may not, except as provided in chapter 47A of this title, be contrary to or inconsistent with this chapter.

(b) All rules and regulations made under this article shall be uniform insofar as practicable, except insofar as applicable to military commissions established under chapter 47A of this title.

§ 837. Art. 37   Unlawfully influencing action of court

(a) No authority convening a general, special, or summary court-martial, nor any other commanding officer, may censure, reprimand, or admonish the court or any member, military judge, or counsel thereof, with respect to the findings or sentence adjudged by the court, or with respect to any other exercise of its or his functions in the conduct of the proceeding. No person subject to this chapter may attempt to coerce or, by any unauthorized means, influence the action of a court-martial or any other military tribunal or any member thereof, in reaching the findings or sentence in any case, or the action of any convening, approving, or reviewing authority with respect to his judicial acts. The foregoing provisions of the subsection shall not apply with respect to (1) general instructional or informational courses in military justice if such courses are designed solely for the purpose of instructing members of a command in the substantive and procedural aspects of courts-martial, or (2) to statements and instructions given in open court by the military judge, president of a special court-martial, or counsel.

(b) In the preparation of an effectiveness, fitness, or efficiency report, or any other report or document used in whole or in part for the purpose of determining whether a member of the armed forces is qualified to be advanced, in grade, or in determining the assignment or transfer of a member of the armed forces or in determining whether a member of the armed forces should be retained on active duty, no person subject to this chapter may, in preparing any such report (1) consider or evaluate the performance of duty of any such member as a member of a court-martial, or (2) give a less favorable rating or evaluation of any member of the armed forces because of the zeal with which such member, as counsel, represented any accused before a court-martial.

§ 838. Art. 38 Duties of trial counsel and defense counsel

(a) The trial counsel of a general or special court-martial shall prosecute in the name of the United States, and shall, under the direction of the court, prepare the record of the proceedings.

(b) (1) The accused has the right to be represented in his defense before a general or special court-martial or at an investigation under section 832 of this title (article 32) as provided in this subsection.

(2) The accused may be represented by civilian counsel if provided by him.

(3) The accused may be represented —

(A) by military counsel detailed under section 827 of this title (article 27); or

(B) by military counsel of his own selection if that counsel is reasonably available (as determined under regulations prescribed under paragraph (7)).

(4) If the accused is represented by civilian counsel, military counsel detailed or selected under paragraph (3) shall act as associate counsel unless excused at the request of the accused.

(5) Except as provided under paragraph (6), if the accused is represented by military counsel of his own selection under paragraph (3)(B), any military counsel detailed under paragraph (3)(A) shall be excused.

(6) The accused is not entitled to be represented by more than one military counsel. However, the person authorized under regulations prescribed under section 827 of this title (article 27) to detail counsel, in his sole discretion —

(A) may detail additional military counsel as assistant defense counsel; and

(B) if the accused is represented by military counsel of his own selection under paragraph (3)(B), may approve a request from the accused that military counsel detailed under paragraph (3)(A) act as associate defense counsel.

(7) The Secretary concerned shall, by regulation, define "reasonably available" for the purpose of paragraph (3)(B) and establish procedures for determining whether the military counsel selected by an accused under that paragraph is reasonably available. Such regulations may not prescribe any limitation based on the reasonable availability of counsel solely on the grounds that the counsel selected by the accused is from an armed force other than the armed force of which the accused is a member. To the maximum extent practicable, such regulations shall establish uniform policies among the armed forces while recognizing the differences in the circumstances and needs of the various armed forces. The Secretary concerned shall submit copies of regulations prescribed under this paragraph to the Committee on Armed Services of the Senate and the Committee on Armed Services of the House of Representatives.

(c) In any court-martial proceeding resulting in a conviction, the defense counsel —

(1) may forward for attachment to the record of proceedings a brief of such matters as he determines should be considered in behalf of the accused on review (including any objection to the contents of the record which he considers appropriate);

(2) may assist the accused in the submission of any matter under section 860 of this title (article 60); and

(3) may take other action authorized by this chapter.

(d) An assistant trial counsel of a general court-martial may, under the direction of the trial counsel or when he is qualified to be a trial counsel as required by section 827 of this title (article 27), perform any duty imposed by law, regulation, or the custom of the service upon the trial counsel of the court. An assistant trial counsel of a special court-martial may perform any duty of the trial counsel.

(e) An assistant defense counsel of a general or special court-martial may, under the direction of the defense counsel or when he is qualified to be the defense counsel as required by section 827 of this title (article 27), perform any duty imposed by law, regulation, or the custom of the service upon counsel for the accused.

§ 839. Art. 39   Sessions

(a) At any time after the service of charges which have been referred for trial to a court-martial composed of a military judge and members, the military judge may, subject to section 835 of this title (article 35), call the court into session without the presence of the members for the purpose of —

(1) hearing and determining motions raising defenses or objections which are capable of determination without trial of the issues raised by a plea of not guilty;

(2) hearing and ruling upon any matter which may be ruled upon by the military judge under this chapter, whether or not the matter is appropriate for later consideration or decision by the members of the court;

(3) if permitted by regulations of the Secretary concerned, holding the arraignment and receiving the pleas of the accused; and

(4) performing any other procedural function which may be performed by the military judge under this chapter or under rules prescribed pursuant to section 836 of this title (article 36) and which does not require the presence of the members of the court.

(b) Proceedings under subsection (a) shall be conducted in the presence of the accused, the defense counsel, and the trial counsel and shall be made a part of the record. These proceedings may be conducted notwithstanding the number of members of the court and without regard to section 829 of this title (article 29). If authorized by regulations of the Secretary concerned, and if at least one defense counsel is physically in the presence of the accused, the presence required by this subsection may otherwise be established by audiovisual technology (such as videoteleconferencing technology).

(c) When the members of a court-martial deliberate or vote, only the members may be present. All other proceedings, including any other consultation of the members of the court with counsel or the military judge, shall be made a part of the record and shall be in the presence of the accused, the defense counsel, the trial counsel, and, in cases in which a military judge has been detailed to the court, the military judge.

(d) The findings, holdings, interpretations, and other precedents of military commissions under chapter 47A of this title —

(1) may not be introduced or considered in any hearing, trial, or other proceeding of a court-martial under this chapter; and

(2) may not form the basis of any holding, decision, or other determination of a court-martial.

§ 840. Art. 40   Continuances

The military judge or a court-martial without a military judge may, for reasonable cause, grant a continuance to any party for such time, and as often, as may appear to be just.

§ 841. Art. 41   Challenges

(a) (1) The military judge and members of a general or special court-martial may be challenged by the accused or the trial counsel for cause stated to the court. The military judge, or, if none, the court, shall determine the relevancy and validity of challenges for cause, and may not receive a challenge to more than one person at a time. Challenges by the trial counsel shall ordinarily be presented and decided before those by the accused are offered.

(2) If exercise of a challenge for cause reduces the court below the minimum number of members required by section 816 of this title (article 16), all parties shall (notwithstanding section 829 of this title (article 29)) either exercise or waive any challenge for cause then apparent against the remaining members of the court before additional members are detailed to the court. However, peremptory challenges shall not be exercised at that time.

(b) (1) Each accused and the trial counsel are entitled initially to one peremptory challenge of members of the court. The military judge may not be challenged except for cause.

(2) If exercise of a peremptory challenge reduces the court below the minimum number of members required by section 816 of this title (article 16), the parties shall (notwithstanding section 829 of this title (article 29)) either exercise or waive any remaining peremptory challenge (not previously waived) against the remaining members of the court before additional members are detailed to the court.

(c) Whenever additional members are detailed to the court, and after any challenges for cause against such additional members are presented and decided, each accused and the trial counsel are entitled to one peremptory challenge against members not previously subject to peremptory challenge.

§ 842. Art. 42   Oaths

(a) Before performing their respective duties, military judges, members of general and special courts-martial, trial counsel, assistant trial counsel, defense counsel, assistant or associate defense counsel, reporters, and interpreters shall take an oath to perform their duties faithfully. The form of the oath, the time and place of the taking thereof, the manner of recording the same, and whether the oath shall be taken for all cases in which these duties are to be performed or for a particular case, shall be as prescribed in regulations of the Secretary concerned. These regulations may provide that an oath to perform faithfully duties as a military judge, trial counsel, assistant trial counsel, defense counsel, or assistant or associate defense counsel may be taken at any time by any judge advocate, or other person certified to be qualified or competent for the duty, and if such an oath is taken it need not again be taken at the time the judge advocate, or other person is detailed to that duty.

(b) Each witness before a court-martial shall be examined on oath.

§ 843. Art. 43   Statute of limitations

(a) A person charged with absence without leave or missing movement in time of war, with murder or rape, or with any other offense punishable by death, may be tried and punished at any time without limitation.

(b) (1) Except as otherwise provided in this section (article), a person charged with an offense is not liable to be tried by court-martial if the offense was committed more than five years before the receipt of sworn charges and specifications by an officer exercising summary court-martial jurisdiction over the command.

(2) (A) A person charged with having committed a child abuse offense against a child is liable to be tried by court-martial if the sworn charges and specifications are received during the life of the child or within five years after the date on which the offense was committed, whichever provides a longer period, by an officer exercising summary court-martial jurisdiction with respect to that person.

(B) In subparagraph (A), the term "child abuse offense" means an act that involves abuse of a person who has not attained the age of 16 years and constitutes any of the following offenses:

(i) Any offense in violation of section 920, 920a, 920b, or 920c of this title (article 120, 120a, 120b, or 120c).

(ii) Maiming in violation of section 924 of this title (article 124).

(iii) Sodomy in violation of section 925 of this title (article 125).

(iv) Aggravated assault or assault consummated by a battery in violation of section 928 of this title (article 128).

(v) Kidnaping, assault with intent to commit murder, voluntary manslaughter, rape, or sodomy, or indecent acts in violation of section 934 of this title (article 134).

(C) In subparagraph (A), the term "child abuse offense" includes an act that involves abuse of a person who has not attained the age of 18 years and would constitute an offense under chapter 110 or 117 of title 18 or under section 1591 of that title 18.

(3) A person charged with an offense is not liable to be punished under section 815 of this title (article 15) if the offense was committed more than two years before the imposition of punishment.

(c) Periods in which the accused is absent without authority or fleeing from justice shall be excluded in computing the period of limitation prescribed in this section (article).

(d) Periods in which the accused was absent from territory in which the United States has the authority to apprehend him, or in the custody of civil authorities, or in the hands of the enemy, shall be excluded in computing the period of limitation prescribed in this article.

(e) For an offense the trial of which in time of war is certified to the President by the Secretary concerned to be detrimental to the prosecution of the war or inimical to the national security, the period of limitation prescribed in this article is extended to six months after the termination of hostilities as proclaimed by the President or by a joint resolution of Congress.

(f) When the United States is at war, the running of any statute of limitations applicable to any offense under this chapter —

(1) involving fraud or attempted fraud against the United States or any agency thereof in any manner, whether by conspiracy or not;

(2) committed in connection with the acquisition, care, handling, custody, control, or disposition of any real or personal property of the United States; or

(3) committed in connection with the negotiation, procurement, award, performance, payment, interim financing, cancellation, or other termination or settlement, of any contract, subcontract, or purchase order which is connected with or related to the prosecution of the war, or with any disposition of termination inventory by any war contractor or Government agency;

is suspended until three years after the termination of hostilities as proclaimed by the President or by a joint resolution of Congress.

(g) (1) If charges or specifications are dismissed as defective or insufficient for any cause and the period prescribed by the applicable statute of limitations —

(A) has expired; or

(B) will expire within 180 days after the date of dismissal of the charges and specifications,

trial and punishment under new charges and specifications are not barred by the statute of limitations if the conditions specified in paragraph (2) are met.

(2) The conditions referred to in paragraph (1) are that the new charges and specifications must —

(A) be received by an officer exercising summary court-martial jurisdiction over the command within 180 days after the dismissal of the charges or specifications; and

(B) allege the same acts or omissions that were alleged in the dismissed charges or specifications (or allege acts or omissions that were included in the dismissed charges or specifications).

§ 844. Art. 44   Former jeopardy

(a) No person may, without his consent, be tried a second time for the same offense.

(b) No proceeding in which an accused has been found guilty by a court-martial upon any charge or specification is a trial in the sense of this article until the finding of guilty has become final after review of the case has been fully completed.

(c) A proceeding which, after the introduction of evidence but before a finding, is dismissed or terminated by the convening authority or on motion of the prosecution for failure of available evidence or witnesses without any fault of the accused is a trial in the sense of this article.

§ 845. Art. 45   Pleas of the accused

(a) If an accused after arraignment makes an irregular pleading, or after a plea of guilty sets up matter inconsistent with the plea, or if it appears that he has entered the plea of guilty improvidently or through lack of understanding of its meaning and effect, or if he fails or refuses to plead, a plea of not guilty shall be entered in the record, and the court shall proceed as though he had pleaded not guilty.

(b) A plea of guilty by the accused may not be received to any charge or specification alleging an offense for which the death penalty may be adjudged. With respect to any other charge or specification to which a plea of guilty has been made by the accused and accepted by the military judge or by a court-martial without a military judge, a finding of guilty of the charge or specification may, if permitted by regulations of the Secretary concerned, be entered immediately without vote. This finding shall constitute the finding of the court unless the plea of guilty is withdrawn prior to announcement of the sentence, in which event the proceedings shall continue as though the accused had pleaded not guilty.

§ 846. Art. 46   Opportunity to obtain witnesses and other evidence

The trial counsel, the defense counsel, and the court-martial shall have equal opportunity to obtain witnesses and other evidence in accordance with such regulations as the President may prescribe. Process issued in court-martial cases to compel witnesses to appear and testify and to compel the production of other evidence shall be similar to that which courts of the United States having criminal jurisdiction may lawfully issue and shall run to any part of the United States, or the Commonwealths and possessions.

§ 847. Art. 47   Refusal to appear or testify

(a) Any person not subject to this chapter who —

(1) has been duly subpoenaed to appear as a witness before a court-martial, military commission, court of inquiry, or any other military court or board, or before any military or civil officer designated to take a deposition to be read in evidence before such a court, commission, or board, or has been duly issued a subpoena duces tecum for an investigation pursuant to section 832(b) of this title (article 32(b));

(2) has been provided a means for reimbursement from the Government for fees and mileage at the rates allowed to witnesses attending the courts of the United States or, in the case of extraordinary hardship is advanced such fees and mileage; and

(3) willfully neglects or refuses to appear, or refuses to qualify as a witness or to testify or to produce any evidence which that person may have been legally subpoenaed to produce;

is guilty of an offense against the United States.

(b) Any person who commits an offense named in subsection (a) shall be tried on indictment or information in a United States district court or in a court of original criminal jurisdiction in any of the Commonwealths or possessions of the United States, and jurisdiction is conferred upon those courts for that purpose. Upon conviction, such a person shall be fined or imprisoned, or both, at the court's discretion.

(c) The United States attorney or the officer prosecuting for the United States in any such court of original criminal jurisdiction shall, upon the certification of the facts to him by the military court, commission, court of inquiry, board, or convening authority, file an information against and prosecute any person violating this article.

(d) The fees and mileage of witnesses shall be advanced or paid out of the appropriations for the compensation of witnesses.

§ 848. Art. 48   Contempts

(a) AUTHORITY TO PUNISH CONTEMPT. — A judge detailed to a court-martial, a court of inquiry, the United States Court of Appeals for the Armed Forces, a military Court of Criminal Appeals, a provost court, or a military commission may punish for contempt any person who —

(1) uses any menacing word, sign, or gesture in the presence of the judge during the proceedings of the court-martial, court, or military commission;

(2) disturbs the proceedings of the court-martial, court, or military commission by any riot or disorder; or

(3) willfully disobeys the lawful writ, process, order, rule, decree, or command of the court-martial, court, or military commission.

(b) PUNISHMENT. — The punishment for contempt under subsection (a) may not exceed confinement for 30 days, a fine of $1,000, or both.

(c) INAPPLICABILITY TO MILITARY COMMISSIONS UNDER CHAPTER 47A. — This section does not apply to a military commission established under chapter 47A of this title.

§ 849. Art. 49   Depositions

(a) At any time after charges have been signed as provided in section 830 of this title (article 30), any party may take oral or written depositions unless the military judge or court-martial without a military judge hearing the case or, if the case is not being heard, an authority competent to convene a court-martial for the trial of those charges forbids it for good cause. If a deposition is to be taken before charges are referred for trial, such an authority may designate commissioned officers to represent the prosecution and the defense and may authorize those officers to take the deposition of any witness.

(b) The party at whose instance a deposition is to be taken shall give to every other party reasonable written notice of the time and place for taking the deposition.

(c) Depositions may be taken before and authenticated by any military or civil officer authorized by the laws of the United States or by the laws of the place where the deposition is taken to administer oaths.

(d) A duly authenticated deposition taken upon reasonable notice to the other parties, so far as otherwise admissible under the rules of evidence, may be read in evidence or, in the case of audiotape, videotape, or similar material, may be played in evidence before any military court or commission in any case not capital, or in any proceeding before a court of inquiry or military board, if it appears —

(1) that the witness resides or is beyond the State, Commonwealth, or District of Columbia in which the court, commission, or board is ordered to sit, or beyond 100 miles from the place of trial or hearing;

(2) that the witness by reason of death, age, sickness, bodily infirmity, imprisonment, military necessity, nonamenability to process, or other reasonable cause, is unable or refuses to appear and testify in person at the place of trial or hearing; or

(3) that the present whereabouts of the witness is unknown.

(e) Subject to subsection (d), testimony by deposition may be presented by the defense in capital cases.

(f) Subject to subsection (d), a deposition may be read in evidence or, in the case of audiotape, videotape, or similar material, may be played in evidence in any case in which the death penalty is authorized but is not mandatory, whenever the convening authority directs that the case be treated as not capital, and in such a case a sentence of death may not be adjudged by the court-martial.

§ 850. Art. 50   Admissibility of records of courts of inquiry

(a) In any case not capital and not extending to the dismissal of a commissioned officer, the sworn testimony, contained in the duly authenticated record of proceedings of a court of inquiry, of a person whose oral testimony cannot be obtained, may, if otherwise admissible under the rules of evidence, be read in evidence by any party before a court-martial or military commission if the accused was a party before the court of inquiry and if the same issue was involved or if the accused consents to the introduction of such evidence. This section does not apply to a military commission established under chapter 47A of this title.

(b) Such testimony may be read in evidence only by the defense in capital cases or cases extending to the dismissal of a commissioned officer.

(c) Such testimony may also be read in evidence before a court of inquiry or a military board.

§ 850a. Art. 50a   Defense of lack of mental responsibility

(a) It is an affirmative defense in a trial by court-martial that, at the time of the commission of the acts constituting the offense, the accused, as a result of a severe mental disease or defect, was unable to appreciate the nature and quality or the wrongfulness of the acts. Mental disease or defect does not otherwise constitute a defense.

(b) The accused has the burden of proving the defense of lack of mental responsibility by clear and convincing evidence.

(c) Whenever lack of mental responsibility of the accused with respect to an offense is properly at issue, the military judge, or the president of a court-martial without a military judge, shall instruct the members of the court as to the defense of lack of mental responsibility under this section and charge them to find the accused —

(1) guilty;

(2) not guilty; or

(3) not guilty only by reason of lack of mental responsibility.

(d) Subsection (c) does not apply to a court-martial composed of a military judge only. In the case of a court-martial composed of a military judge only, whenever lack of mental responsibility of the accused with respect to an offense is properly at issue, the military judge shall find the accused —

(1) guilty;

(2) not guilty; or

(3) not guilty only by reason of lack of mental responsibility.

(e) Notwithstanding the provisions of section 852 of this title (article 52), the accused shall be found not guilty only by reason of lack of mental responsibility if —

(1) a majority of the members of the court-martial present at the time the vote is taken determines that the defense of lack of mental responsibility has been established; or

(2) in the case of a court-martial composed of a military judge only, the military judge determines that the defense of lack of mental responsibility has been established.

§ 851. Art. 51   Voting and rulings

(a) Voting by members of a general or special court-martial on the findings and on the sentence, and by members of a court-martial without a military judge upon questions of challenge, shall be by secret written ballot. The junior member of the court shall count the votes. The count shall be checked by the president, who shall forthwith announce the result of the ballot to the members of the court.

(b) The military judge and, except for questions of challenge, the president of a court-martial without a military judge shall rule upon all questions of law and all interlocutory questions arising during the proceedings. Any such ruling made by the military judge upon any question of law or any interlocutory question other than the factual issue of mental responsibility of the accused, or by the president of a court-martial without a military judge upon any question of law other than a motion for a finding of not guilty, is final and constitutes the ruling of the court. However, the military judge or the president of a court-martial without a military judge may change his ruling at any time during the trial. Unless the ruling is final, if any member objects thereto, the court shall be cleared and closed and the question decided by a voice vote as provided in section 852 of this title (article 52), beginning with the junior in rank.

(c) Before a vote is taken on the findings, the military judge or the president of a court-martial without a military judge shall, in the presence of the accused and counsel, instruct the members of the court as to the elements of the offense and charge them —

(1) that the accused must be presumed to be innocent until his guilt is established by legal and competent evidence beyond reasonable doubt;

(2) that in the case being considered, if there is a reasonable doubt as to the guilt of the accused, the doubt must be resolved in favor of the accused and he must be acquitted;

(3) that, if there is a reasonable doubt as to the degree of guilt, the finding must be in a lower degree as to which there is no reasonable doubt; and

(4) that the burden of proof to establish the guilt of the accused beyond reasonable doubt is upon the United States.

(d) Subsections (a), (b), and (c) do not apply to a court-martial composed of a military judge only. The military judge of such a court-martial shall determine all questions of law and fact arising during the proceedings and, if the accused is convicted, adjudge an appropriate sentence. The military judge of such a court-martial shall make a general finding and shall in addition on request find the facts specially. If an opinion or memorandum of decision is filed, it will be sufficient if the findings of fact appear therein.

§ 852. Art. 52   Number of votes required

(a) (1) No person may be convicted of an offense for which the death penalty is made mandatory by law, except by the concurrence of all the members of the court-martial present at the time the vote is taken.

(2) No person may be convicted of any other offense, except as provided in section 845(b) of this title (article 45(b)) or by the concurrence of two-thirds of the members present at the time the vote is taken.

(b) (1) No person may be sentenced to suffer death, except by the concurrence of all the members of the court-martial present at the time the vote is taken and for an offense in this chapter expressly made punishable by death.

(2) No person may be sentenced to life imprisonment or to confinement for more than ten years, except by the concurrence of three-fourths of the members present at the time the vote is taken.

(3) All other sentences shall be determined by the concurrence of two-thirds of the members present at the time the vote is taken.

(c) All other questions to be decided by the members of a general or special court-martial shall be determined by a majority vote, but a determination to reconsider a finding of guilty or to reconsider a sentence, with a view toward decreasing it, may be made by any lesser vote which indicates that the reconsideration is not opposed by the number of votes required for that finding or sentence. A tie vote on a challenge disqualifies the member challenged. A tie vote on a motion for a finding of not guilty or on a motion relating to the question of the accused's sanity is a determination against the accused. A tie vote on any other question is a determination in favor of the accused.

§ 853. Art. 53   Court to announce action

A court-martial shall announce its findings and sentence to the parties as soon as determined.

§ 854. Art. 54   Record of trial

(a) Each general court-martial shall keep a separate record of the proceedings in each case brought before it, and the record shall be authenticated by the signature of the military judge. If the record cannot be authenticated by the military judge by reason of his death, disability, or absence, it shall be authenticated by the signature of the trial counsel or by that of a member if the trial counsel is unable to authenticate it by reason of his death, disability, or absence. In a court-martial consisting of only a military judge the record shall be authenticated by the court reporter under the same conditions which would impose such a duty on a member under this subsection.

(b) Each special and summary court-martial shall keep a separate record of the proceedings in each case, and the record shall be authenticated in the manner required by such regulations as the President may prescribe.

(c) (1) A complete record of the proceedings and testimony shall be prepared —

(A) in each general court-martial case in which the sentence adjudged includes death, a dismissal, a discharge, or (if the sentence adjudged does not include a discharge) any other punishment which exceeds that which may otherwise be adjudged by a special court-martial; and

(B) in each special court-martial case in which the sentence adjudged includes a bad-conduct discharge, confinement for more than six months, or forfeiture of pay for more than six months.

(2) In all other court-martial cases, the record shall contain such matters as may be prescribed by regulations of the President.

(d) A copy of the record of the proceedings of each general and special court-martial shall be given to the accused as soon as it is authenticated.

SUBCHAPTER VIII.   SENTENCES

§ 855. Art. 55   Cruel and unusual punishments prohibited

Punishment by flogging, or by branding, marking, or tattooing on the body, or any other cruel or unusual punishment, may not be adjudged by any court-martial or inflicted upon any person subject to this chapter. The use of irons, single or double, except for the purpose of safe custody, is prohibited.

§ 856. Art. 56   Maximum limits

The punishment which a court-martial may direct for an offense may not exceed such limits as the President may prescribe for that offense.

§ 856a. Art. 56a   Sentence of confinement for life without eligibility for parole

(a) For any offense for which a sentence of confinement for life may be adjudged, a court-martial may adjudge a sentence of confinement for life without eligibility for parole.

(b) An accused who is sentenced to confinement for life without eligibility for parole shall be confined for the remainder of the accused's life unless —

(1) the sentence is set aside or otherwise modified as a result of —

(A) action taken by the convening authority, the Secretary concerned, or another person authorized to act under section 860 of this title (article 60); or

(B) any other action taken during post-trial procedure and review under any other provision of subchapter IX;

(2) the sentence is set aside or otherwise modified as a result of action taken by a Court of Criminal Appeals, the Court of Appeals for the Armed Forces, or the Supreme Court; or

(3) the accused is pardoned.

§ 857. Art. 57   Effective date of sentences

(a) (1) Any forfeiture of pay or allowances or reduction in grade that is included in a sentence of a court-martial takes effect on the earlier of —

(A) the date that is 14 days after the date on which the sentence is adjudged; or

(B) the date on which the sentence is approved by the convening authority.

(2) On application by an accused, the convening authority may defer a forfeiture of pay or allowances or reduction in grade that would otherwise become effective under paragraph (1)(A) until the date on which the sentence is approved by the convening authority. Such a deferment may be rescinded at any time by the convening authority.

(3) A forfeiture of pay or allowances shall be applicable to pay and allowances accruing on and after the date on which the sentence takes effect.

(4) In this subsection, the term "convening authority", with respect to a sentence of a court-martial, means any person authorized to act on the sentence under section 860 of this title (article 60).

(b) Any period of confinement included in a sentence of a court-martial begins to run from the date the sentence is adjudged by the court-martial, but periods during which the sentence to confinement is suspended or deferred shall be excluded in computing the service of the term of confinement.

(c) All other sentences of courts-martial are effective on the date ordered executed.

§ 857a. Art. 57a   Deferment of sentences

(a) On application by an accused who is under sentence to confinement that has not been ordered executed, the convening authority or, if the accused is no longer under his jurisdiction, the officer exercising general court-martial jurisdiction over the command to which the accused is currently assigned, may in his sole discretion defer service of the sentence to confinement. The deferment shall terminate when the sentence is ordered executed. The deferment may be rescinded at any time by the officer who granted it or, if the accused is no longer under his jurisdiction, by the officer exercising general court-martial jurisdiction over the command to which the accused is currently assigned.

(b) (1) In any case in which a court-martial sentences a person referred to in paragraph (2) to confinement, the convening authority may defer the service of the sentence to confinement, without the consent of that person, until after the person has been permanently released to the armed forces by a State or foreign country referred to in that paragraph.

(2) Paragraph (1) applies to a person subject to this chapter who —

(A) while in the custody of a State or foreign country is temporarily returned by that State or foreign country to the armed forces for trial by court-martial; and

(B) after the court-martial, is returned to that State or foreign country under the authority of a mutual agreement or treaty, as the case may be.

(3) In this subsection, the term "State" includes the District of Columbia and any commonwealth, territory, or possession of the United States.

(c) In any case in which a court-martial sentences a person to confinement and the sentence to confinement has been ordered executed, but in which review of the case under section 867(a)(2) of this title (article 67(a)(2)) is pending, the Secretary concerned may defer further service of the sentence to confinement while that review is pending.

§ 858. Art. 58   Execution of confinement

(a) Under such instructions as the Secretary concerned may prescribe, a sentence of confinement adjudged by a court-martial or other military tribunal, whether or not the sentence includes discharge or dismissal, and whether or not the discharge or dismissal has been executed, may be carried into execution by confinement in any place of confinement under the control of any of the armed forces or in any penal or correctional institution under the control of the United States, or which the United States may be allowed to use. Persons so confined in a penal or correctional institution not under the control of one of the armed forces are subject to the same discipline and treatment as persons confined or committed by the courts of the United States or of the State, District of Columbia, or place in which the institution is situated.

(b) The omission of the words "hard labor" from any sentence of a court-martial adjudging confinement does not deprive the authority executing that sentence of the power to require hard labor as a part of the punishment.

§ 858a. Art. 58a   Sentences: reduction in enlisted grade upon approval

(a) Unless otherwise provided in regulations to be prescribed by the Secretary concerned, a court-martial sentence of an enlisted member in a pay grade above E-1, as approved by the convening authority, that includes —

(1) a dishonorable or bad-conduct discharge;

(2) confinement; or

(3) hard labor without confinement;

reduces that member to pay grade E-1, effective on the date of that approval.

(b) If the sentence of a member who is reduced in pay grade under subsection (a) is set aside or disapproved, or, as finally approved, does not include any punishment named in subsection (a)(1), (2), or (3), the rights and privileges of which he was deprived because of that reduction shall be restored to him and he is entitled to the pay and allowances to which he would have been entitled, for the period the reduction was in effect, had he not been so reduced.

§ 858b. Art. 58b   Sentences: forfeiture of pay and allowances during confinement

(a) (1) A court-martial sentence described in paragraph (2) shall result in the forfeiture of pay, or of pay and allowances, due that member during any period of confinement or parole. The forfeiture pursuant to this section shall take effect on the date determined under section 857(a) of this title (article 57(a)) and may be deferred as provided by that section. The pay and allowances forfeited, in the case of a general court-martial, shall be all pay and allowances due that member during such period and, in the case of a special court-martial, shall be two-thirds of all pay due that member during such period.

(2) A sentence covered by this section is any sentence that includes —

(A) confinement for more than six months or death; or

(B) confinement for six months or less and a dishonorable or bad-conduct discharge or dismissal.

(b) In a case involving an accused who has dependents, the convening authority or other person acting under section 860 of this title (article 60) may waive any or all of the forfeitures of pay and allowances required by subsection (a) for a period not to exceed six months. Any amount of pay or allowances that, except for a waiver under this subsection, would be forfeited shall be paid, as the convening authority or other person taking action directs, to the dependents of the accused.

(c) If the sentence of a member who forfeits pay and allowances under subsection (a) is set aside or disapproved or, as finally approved, does not provide for a punishment referred to in subsection (a)(2), the member shall be paid the pay and allowances which the member would have been paid, except for the forfeiture, for the period during which the forfeiture was in effect.

SUBCHAPTER IX.   POST-TRIAL PROCEDURE AND REVIEW OF COURTS-MARTIAL

§ 859. Art. 59   Error of law; lesser included offense

(a) A finding or sentence of a court-martial may not be held incorrect on the ground of an error of law unless the error materially prejudices the substantial rights of the accused.

(b) Any reviewing authority with the power to approve or affirm a finding of guilty may approve or affirm, instead, so much of the finding as includes a lesser included offense.

§ 860. Art. 60   Action by the convening authority

(a) The findings and sentence of a court-martial shall be reported promptly to the convening authority after the announcement of the sentence.

(b) (1) The accused may submit to the convening authority matters for consideration by the convening authority with respect to the findings and the sentence. Any such submission shall be in writing. Except in a summary court-martial case, such a submission shall be made within 10 days after the accused has been given an authenticated record of trial and, if applicable, the recommendation of the staff judge advocate or legal officer under subsection (d). In a summary court-martial case, such a submission shall be made within seven days after the sentence is announced.

(2) If the accused shows that additional time is required for the accused to submit such matters, the convening authority or other person taking action under this section, for good cause, may extend the applicable period under paragraph (1) for not more than an additional 20 days.

(3) In a summary court-martial case, the accused shall be promptly provided a copy of the record of trial for use in preparing a submission authorized by paragraph (1).

(4) The accused may waive his right to make a submission to the convening authority under paragraph (1). Such a waiver must be made in writing and may not be revoked. For the purposes of subsection (c)(2), the time within which the accused may make a submission under this subsection shall be deemed to have expired upon the submission of such a waiver to the convening authority.

(c) (1) The authority under this section to modify the findings and sentence of a court-martial is a matter of command prerogative involving the sole discretion of the convening authority. Under regulations of the Secretary concerned, a commissioned officer commanding for the time being, a successor in command, or any person exercising general court-martial jurisdiction may act under this section in place of the convening authority.

(2) Action on the sentence of a court-martial shall be taken by the convening authority or by another person authorized to act under this section. Subject to regulations of the Secretary concerned, such action may be taken only after consideration of any matters submitted by the accused under subsection (b) or

after the time for submitting such matters expires, whichever is earlier. The convening authority or other person taking such action, in his sole discretion, may approve, disapprove, commute, or suspend the sentence in whole or in part.

(3) Action on the findings of a court-martial by the convening authority or other person acting on the sentence is not required. However, such person, in his sole discretion may —

(A) dismiss any charge or specification by setting aside a finding of guilty thereto; or

(B) change a finding of guilty to a charge or specification to a finding of guilty to an offense that is a lesser included offense of the offense stated in the charge or specification.

(d) Before acting under this section on any general court-martial case or any special court-martial case that includes a bad-conduct discharge, the convening authority or other person taking action under this section shall obtain and consider the written recommendation of his staff judge advocate or legal officer. The convening authority or other person taking action under this section shall refer the record of trial to his staff judge advocate or legal officer, and the staff judge advocate or legal officer shall use such record in the preparation of his recommendation. The recommendation of the staff judge advocate or legal officer shall include such matters as the President may prescribe by regulation and shall be served on the accused, who may submit any matter in response under subsection (b). Failure to object in the response to the recommendation or to any matter attached to the recommendation waives the right to object thereto.

(e) (1) The convening authority or other person taking action under this section, in his sole discretion, may order a proceeding in revision or a rehearing.

(2) A proceeding in revision may be ordered if there is an apparent error or omission in the record or if the record shows improper or inconsistent action by a court-martial with respect to the findings or sentence that can be rectified without material prejudice to the substantial rights of the accused. In no case, however, may a proceeding in revision —

(A) reconsider a finding of not guilty of any specification or a ruling which amounts to a finding of not guilty;

(B) reconsider a finding of not guilty of any charge, unless there has been a finding of guilty under a specification laid under that charge, which sufficiently alleges a violation of some article of this chapter; or

(C) increase the severity of the sentence unless the sentence prescribed for the offense is mandatory.

(3) A rehearing may be ordered by the convening authority or other person taking action under this section if he disapproves the findings and sentence and states the reasons for disapproval of the findings. If such person disapproves the findings and sentence and does not order a rehearing, he shall

dismiss the charges. A rehearing as to the findings may not be ordered where there is a lack of sufficient evidence in the record to support the findings. A rehearing as to the sentence may be ordered if the convening authority or other person taking action under this subsection disapproves the sentence.

§ 861. Art. 61   Waiver or withdrawal of appeal

(a) In each case subject to appellate review under section 866 or 869(a) of this title (article 66 or 69(a)), except a case in which the sentence as approved under section 860(c) of this title (article 60(c)) includes death, the accused may file with the convening authority a statement expressly waiving the right of the accused to such review. Such a waiver shall be signed by both the accused and by defense counsel and must be filed within 10 days after the action under section 860(c) of this title (article 60(c)) is served on the accused or on defense counsel. The convening authority or other person taking such action, for good cause, may extend the period for such filing by not more than 30 days.

(b) Except in a case in which the sentence as approved under section 860(c) of this title (article 60(c)) includes death, the accused may withdraw an appeal at any time.

(c) A waiver of the right to appellate review or the withdrawal of an appeal under this section bars review under section 866 or 869(a) of this title (article 66 or 69(a)).

§ 862. Art. 62   Appeal by the United States

(a) (1) In a trial by court-martial in which a military judge presides and in which a punitive discharge may be adjudged, the United States may appeal the following (other than an order or ruling that is, or that amounts to, a finding of not guilty with respect to the charge or specification):

(A) An order or ruling of the military judge which terminates the proceedings with respect to a charge or specification.

(B) An order or ruling which excludes evidence that is substantial proof of a fact material in the proceeding.

(C) An order or ruling which directs the disclosure of classified information.

(D) An order or ruling which imposes sanctions for nondisclosure of classified information.

(E) A refusal of the military judge to issue a protective order sought by the United States to prevent the disclosure of classified information.

(F) A refusal by the military judge to enforce an order described in subparagraph (E) that has previously been issued by appropriate authority.

(2) An appeal of an order or ruling may not be taken unless the trial counsel provides the military judge with written notice of appeal from the order or ruling within 72 hours of the order or ruling. Such notice shall include a certification by the trial counsel that the appeal is not taken for the purpose of

delay and (if the order or ruling appealed is one which excludes evidence) that the evidence excluded is substantial proof of a fact material in the proceeding.

(3) An appeal under this section shall be diligently prosecuted by appellate Government counsel.

(b) An appeal under this section shall be forwarded by a means prescribed under regulations of the President directly to the Court of Criminal Appeals and shall, whenever practicable, have priority over all other proceedings before that court. In ruling on an appeal under this section, the Court of Criminal Appeals may act only with respect to matters of law, notwithstanding section 866(c) of this title (article 66(c)).

(c) Any period of delay resulting from an appeal under this section shall be excluded in deciding any issue regarding denial of a speedy trial unless an appropriate authority determines that the appeal was filed solely for the purpose of delay with the knowledge that it was totally frivolous and without merit.

§ 863. Art. 63   Rehearings

Each rehearing under this chapter shall take place before a court-martial composed of members not members of the court-martial which first heard the case. Upon a rehearing the accused may not be tried for any offense of which he was found not guilty by the first court-martial, and no sentence in excess of or more severe than the original sentence may be approved, unless the sentence is based upon a finding of guilty of an offense not considered upon the merits in the original proceedings, or unless the sentence prescribed for the offense is mandatory. If the sentence approved after the first court-martial was in accordance with a pretrial agreement and the accused at the rehearing changes his plea with respect to the charges or specifications upon which the pretrial agreement was based, or otherwise does not comply with the pretrial agreement, the approved sentence as to those charges or specifications may include any punishment not in excess of that lawfully adjudged at the first court-martial.

§ 864. Art. 64   Review by a judge advocate

(a) Each case in which there has been a finding of guilty that is not reviewed under section 866 or 869(a) of this title (article 66 or 69(a)) shall be reviewed by a judge advocate under regulations of the Secretary concerned. A judge advocate may not review a case under this subsection if he has acted in the same case as an accuser, investigating officer, member of the court, military judge, or counsel or has otherwise acted on behalf of the prosecution or defense. The judge advocate's review shall be in writing and shall contain the following:

(1) Conclusions as to whether —

(A) the court had jurisdiction over the accused and the offense;

(B) the charge and specification stated an offense; and

(C) the sentence was within the limits prescribed as a matter of law.

(2) A response to each allegation of error made in writing by the accused.

(3) If the case is sent for action under subsection (b), a recommendation as to the appropriate action to be taken and an opinion as to whether corrective action is required as a matter of law.

(b) The record of trial and related documents in each case reviewed under subsection (a) shall be sent for action to the person exercising general court-martial jurisdiction over the accused at the time the court was convened (or to that person's successor in command) if —

(1) the judge advocate who reviewed the case recommends corrective action;

(2) the sentence approved under section 860(c) of this title (article 60(c)) extends to dismissal, a bad-conduct or dishonorable discharge, or confinement for more than six months; or

(3) such action is otherwise required by regulations of the Secretary concerned.

(c) (1) The person to whom the record of trial and related documents are sent under subsection (b) may —

(A) disapprove or approve the findings or sentence, in whole or in part;

(B) remit, commute, or suspend the sentence in whole or in part;

(C) except where the evidence was insufficient at the trial to support the findings, order a rehearing on the findings, on the sentence, or on both; or

(D) dismiss the charges.

(2) If a rehearing is ordered but the convening authority finds a rehearing impracticable, he shall dismiss the charges.

(3) If the opinion of the judge advocate in the judge advocate's review under subsection (a) is that corrective action is required as a matter of law and if the person required to take action under subsection (b) does not take action that is at least as favorable to the accused as that recommended by the judge advocate, the record of trial and action thereon shall be sent to the Judge Advocate General for review under section 869(b) of this title (article 69(b)).

§ 865. Art. 65 Disposition of records

(a) In a case subject to appellate review under section 866 or 869(a) of this title (article 66 or 69(a)) in which the right to such review is not waived, or an appeal is not withdrawn, under section 861 of this title (article 61), the record of trial and action thereon shall be transmitted to the Judge Advocate General for appropriate action.

(b) Except as otherwise required by this chapter, all other records of trial and related documents shall be transmitted and disposed of as the Secretary concerned may prescribe by regulation.

§ 866. Art. 66 Review by Court of Criminal Appeals

(a) Each Judge Advocate General shall establish a Court of Criminal Appeals which shall be composed of one or more panels, and each such panel shall be composed of not less than three appellate military judges. For the purpose of reviewing court-martial cases, the court may sit in panels or as a whole in accordance with rules prescribed under subsection (f). Any decision of a panel may be reconsidered by the court sitting as a whole in accordance with such rules. Appellate military judges who are assigned to a Court of Criminal Appeals may be commissioned officers or civilians, each of whom must be a member of a bar of a Federal court or of the highest court of a State. The Judge Advocate General shall designate as chief judge one of the appellate military judges of the Court of Criminal Appeals established by him. The chief judge shall determine on which panels of the court the appellate judges assigned to the court will serve and which military judge assigned to the court will act as the senior judge on each panel.

(b) The Judge Advocate General shall refer to a Court of Criminal Appeals the record in each case of trial by court-martial —

(1) in which the sentence, as approved, extends to death, dismissal of a commissioned officer, cadet, or midshipman, dishonorable or bad-conduct discharge, or confinement for one year or more; and

(2) except in the case of a sentence extending to death, the right to appellate review has not been waived or an appeal has not been withdrawn under section 861 of this title (article 61).

(c) In a case referred to it, the Court of Criminal Appeals may act only with respect to the findings and sentence as approved by the convening authority. It may affirm only such findings of guilty, and the sentence or such part or amount of the sentence, as it finds correct in law and fact and determines, on the basis of the entire record, should be approved. In considering the record, it may weigh the evidence, judge the credibility of witnesses, and determine controverted questions of fact, recognizing that the trial court saw and heard the witnesses.

(d) If the Court of Criminal Appeals sets aside the findings and sentence, it may, except where the setting aside is based on lack of sufficient evidence in the record to support the findings, order a rehearing. If it sets aside the findings and sentence and does not order a rehearing, it shall order that the charges be dismissed.

(e) The Judge Advocate General shall, unless there is to be further action by the President, the Secretary concerned, the Court of Appeals for the Armed Forces, or the Supreme Court, instruct the convening authority to take action in accordance with the decision of the Court of Criminal Appeals. If the Court of Appeals for the Armed Forces has ordered a rehearing but the convening authority finds a rehearing impracticable, he may dismiss the charges.

(f) The Judge Advocates General shall prescribe uniform rules of procedure for Courts of Criminal Appeals and shall meet periodically to formulate policies and procedure in regard to review of court-martial cases in the offices of the Judge Advocates General and by Courts of Criminal Appeals.

(g) No member of a Court of Criminal Appeals shall be required, or on his own initiative be permitted, to prepare, approve, disapprove, review, or submit, with respect to any other member of the same or another Court of Criminal Appeals, an effectiveness, fitness, or efficiency report, or any other report or document used in whole or in part for the purpose of determining whether a member of the armed forces is qualified to be advanced in grade, or in determining the assignment or transfer of a member of the armed forces, or in determining whether a member of the armed forces should be retained on active duty.

(h) No member of a Court of Criminal Appeals shall be eligible to review the record of any trial if such member served as investigating officer in the case or served as a member of the court-martial before which such trial was conducted, or served as military judge, trial or defense counsel, or reviewing officer of such trial.

§ 867. Art. 67   Review by the Court of Appeals for the Armed Forces

(a) The Court of Appeals for the Armed Forces shall review the record in —

(1) all cases in which the sentence, as affirmed by a Court of Criminal Appeals, extends to death;

(2) all cases reviewed by a Court of Criminal Appeals which the Judge Advocate General orders sent to the Court of Appeals for the Armed Forces for review; and

(3) all cases reviewed by a Court of Criminal Appeals in which, upon petition of the accused and on good cause shown, the Court of Appeals for the Armed Forces has granted a review.

(b) The accused may petition the Court of Appeals for the Armed Forces for review of a decision of a Court of Criminal Appeals within 60 days from the earlier of —

(1) the date on which the accused is notified of the decision of the Court of Criminal Appeals; or

(2) the date on which a copy of the decision of the Court of Criminal Appeals, after being served on appellate counsel of record for the accused (if any), is deposited in the United States mails for delivery by first-class certified mail to the accused at an address provided by the accused or, if no such address has been provided by the accused, at the latest address listed for the accused in his official service record.

The Court of Appeals for the Armed Forces shall act upon such a petition promptly in accordance with the rules of the court.

(c) In any case reviewed by it, the Court of Appeals for the Armed Forces may act only with respect to the findings and sentence as approved by the convening authority and as affirmed or set aside as incorrect in law by the Court of Criminal Appeals. In a case which the Judge Advocate General orders sent to the Court of Appeals for the Armed Forces, that action need be taken only with respect to the issues raised by him. In a case reviewed upon petition of the accused, that action need be taken only with respect to issues specified in the grant of review. The Court of Appeals for the Armed Forces shall take action only with respect to matters of law.

(d) If the Court of Appeals for the Armed Forces sets aside the findings and sentence, it may, except where the setting aside is based on lack of sufficient evidence in the record to support the findings, order a rehearing. If it sets aside the findings and sentence and does not order a rehearing, it shall order that the charges be dismissed.

(e) After it has acted on a case, the Court of Appeals for the Armed Forces may direct the Judge Advocate General to return the record to the Court of Criminal Appeals for further review in accordance with the decision of the court. Otherwise, unless there is to be further action by the President or the Secretary concerned, the Judge Advocate General shall instruct the convening authority to take action in accordance with that decision. If the court has ordered a rehearing, but the convening authority finds a rehearing impracticable, he may dismiss the charges.

§ 867a. Art. 67a   Review by the Supreme Court

(a) Decisions of the United States Court of Appeals for the Armed Forces are subject to review by the Supreme Court by writ of certiorari as provided in section 1259 of title 28. The Supreme Court may not review by a writ of certiorari under this section any action of the Court of Appeals for the Armed Forces in refusing to grant a petition for review.

(b) The accused may petition the Supreme Court for a writ of certiorari without prepayment of fees and costs or security therefor and without filing the affidavit required by section 1915(a) of title 28.

§ 868. Art. 68   Branch offices

The Secretary concerned may direct the Judge Advocate General to establish a branch office with any command. The branch office shall be under an Assistant Judge Advocate General who, with the consent of the Judge Advocate General, may establish a Court of Criminal Appeals with one or more panels. That Assistant Judge Advocate General and any Court of Criminal Appeals established by him may perform for that command under the general supervision of the Judge Advocate General, the respective duties which the Judge Advocate General and a Court of Criminal Appeals established by the Judge Advocate General would otherwise be required to perform as to all cases involving sentences not requiring approval by the President.

§ 869. Art. 69   Review in the office of the Judge Advocate General

(a) The record of trial in each general court-martial that is not otherwise reviewed under section 866 of this title (article 66) shall be examined in the office of the Judge Advocate General if there is a finding of guilty and the accused does not waive or withdraw his right to appellate review under section 861 of this title (article 61). If any part of the findings or sentence is found to be unsupported in law or if reassessment of the sentence is appropriate, the Judge Advocate General may modify or set aside the findings or sentence or both.

(b) The findings or sentence, or both, in a court-martial case not reviewed under subsection (a) or under section 866 of this title (article 66) may be modified or set aside, in whole or in part, by the Judge Advocate General on the ground of newly discovered evidence, fraud on the court, lack of jurisdiction over the accused or the offense, error prejudicial to the substantial rights of the accused, or the appropriateness of the sentence. If such a case is considered upon application of the accused, the application must be filed in the office of the Judge Advocate General by the accused on or before the last day of the two-year period beginning on the date the sentence is approved under section 860(c) of this title (article 60(c)), unless the accused establishes good cause for failure to file within that time.

(c) If the Judge Advocate General sets aside the findings or sentence, he may, except when the setting aside is based on lack of sufficient evidence in the record to support the findings, order a rehearing. If he sets aside the findings and sentence and does not order a rehearing, he shall order that the charges be dismissed. If the Judge Advocate General orders a rehearing but the convening authority finds a rehearing impractical, the convening authority shall dismiss the charges.

(d) A Court of Criminal Appeals may review, under section 866 of this title (article 66) —

(1) any court-martial case which (A) is subject to action by the Judge Advocate General under this section, and (B) is sent to the Court of Criminal Appeals by order of the Judge Advocate General; and

(2) any action taken by the Judge Advocate General under this section in such case.

(e) Notwithstanding section 866 of this title (article 66), in any case reviewed by a Court of Criminal Appeals under this section, the Court may take action only with respect to matters of law.

§ 870. Art. 70 Appellate counsel

(a) The Judge Advocate General shall detail in his office one or more commissioned officers as appellate Government counsel, and one or more commissioned officers as appellate defense counsel, who are qualified under section 827(b)(1) of this title (article 27(b)(1)).

(b) Appellate Government counsel shall represent the United States before the Court of Criminal Appeals or the Court of Appeals for the Armed Forces when directed to do so by the Judge Advocate General. Appellate Government counsel may represent the United States before the Supreme Court in cases arising under this chapter when requested to do so by the Attorney General.

(c) Appellate defense counsel shall represent the accused before the Court of Criminal Appeals, the Court of Appeals for the Armed Forces, or the Supreme Court —

(1) when requested by the accused;

(2) when the United States is represented by counsel; or

(3) when the Judge Advocate General has sent the case to the Court of

Appeals for the Armed Forces.

(d) The accused has the right to be represented before the Court of Criminal Appeals, the Court of Appeals for the Armed Forces, or the Supreme Court by civilian counsel if provided by him.

(e) Military appellate counsel shall also perform such other functions in connection with the review of court martial cases as the Judge Advocate General directs.

§ 871. Art. 71   Execution of sentence; suspension of sentence

(a) If the sentence of the court-martial extends to death, that part of the sentence providing for death may not be executed until approved by the President. In such a case, the President may commute, remit, or suspend the sentence, or any part thereof, as he sees fit. That part of the sentence providing for death may not be suspended.

(b) If in the case of a commissioned officer, cadet, or midshipman, the sentence of a court-martial extends to dismissal, that part of the sentence providing for dismissal may not be executed until approved by the Secretary concerned or such Under Secretary or Assistant Secretary as may be designated by the Secretary concerned. In such a case, the Secretary, Under Secretary, or Assistant Secretary, as the case may be, may commute, remit, or suspend the sentence, or any part of the sentence, as he sees fit. In time of war or national emergency he may commute a sentence of dismissal to reduction to any enlisted grade. A person so reduced may be required to serve for the duration of the war or emergency and six months thereafter.

(c) (1) If a sentence extends to death, dismissal, or a dishonorable or bad-conduct discharge and if the right of the accused to appellate review is not waived, and an appeal is not withdrawn, under section 861 of this title (article 61), that part of the sentence extending to death, dismissal, or a dishonorable or bad-conduct discharge may not be executed until there is a final judgment as to the legality of the proceedings (and with respect to death or dismissal, approval under subsection (a) or (b), as appropriate). A judgment as to legality of the proceedings is final in such cases when review is completed by a Court of Criminal Appeals and —

(A) the time for the accused to file a petition for review by the Court of Appeals for the Armed Forces has expired and the accused has not filed a timely petition for such review and the case is not otherwise under review by that Court;

(B) such a petition is rejected by the Court of Appeals for the Armed Forces; or

(C) review is completed in accordance with the judgment of the Court of Appeals for the Armed Forces and —

(i) a petition for a writ of certiorari is not filed within the time limits prescribed by the Supreme Court;

(ii) such a petition is rejected by the Supreme Court; or

(iii) review is otherwise completed in accordance with the judgment of the Supreme Court.

(2) If a sentence extends to dismissal or a dishonorable or bad conduct discharge and if the right of the accused to appellate review is waived, or an appeal is withdrawn, under section 861 of this title (article 61), that part of the sentence extending to dismissal or a bad-conduct or dishonorable discharge may not be executed until review of the case by a judge advocate (and any action on that review) under section 864 of this title (article 64) is completed. Any other part of a court-martial sentence may be ordered executed by the convening authority or other person acting on the case under section 860 of this title (article 60) when approved by him under that section.

(d) The convening authority or other person acting on the case under section 860 of this title (article 60) may suspend the execution of any sentence or part thereof, except a death sentence.

§ 872. Art. 72   Vacation of suspension

(a) Before the vacation of the suspension of a special court-martial sentence which as approved includes a bad-conduct discharge, or of any general court-martial sentence, the officer having special court-martial jurisdiction over the probationer shall hold a hearing on the alleged violation of probation. The probationer shall be represented at the hearing by counsel if he so desires.

(b) The record of the hearing and the recommendation of the officer having special court-martial jurisdiction shall be sent for action to the officer exercising general court-martial jurisdiction over the probationer. If he vacates the suspension, any unexecuted part of the sentence, except a dismissal, shall be executed, subject to applicable restrictions in section 871(c) of this title (article 71(c)). The vacation of the suspension of a dismissal is not effective until approved by the Secretary concerned.

(c) The suspension of any other sentence may be vacated by any authority competent to convene, for the command in which the accused is serving or assigned, a court of the kind that imposed the sentence.

§ 873. Art. 73   Petition for a new trial

At any time within two years after approval by the convening authority of a court-martial sentence, the accused may petition the Judge Advocate General for a new trial on the grounds of newly discovered evidence or fraud on the court. If the accused's case is pending before a Court of Criminal Appeals or before the Court of Appeals for the Armed Forces, the Judge Advocate General shall refer the petition to the appropriate court for action. Otherwise the Judge Advocate General shall act upon the petition.

§ 874. Art. 74   Remission and suspension

(a) The Secretary concerned and, when designated by him, any Under Secretary, Assistant Secretary, Judge Advocate General, or commanding officer may remit or suspend any part or amount of the unexecuted part of any sentence, including all uncollected forfeitures other than a sentence approved by the President. However, in the case of a sentence of confinement for life without eligibility for parole that is adjudged for an offense committed after October 29, 2000, after the sentence is ordered executed, the authority of the Secretary concerned under the preceding sentence (1) may not be delegated, and (2) may be exercised only after the service of a period of confinement of not less than 20 years.

(b) The Secretary concerned may, for good cause, substitute an administrative form of discharge for a discharge or dismissal executed in accordance with the sentence of a court-martial.

§ 875. Art. 75   Restoration

(a) Under such regulations as the President may prescribe, all rights, privileges, and property affected by an executed part of a court-martial sentence which has been set aside or disapproved, except an executed dismissal or discharge, shall be restored unless a new trial or rehearing is ordered and such executed part is included in a sentence imposed upon the new trial or rehearing.

(b) If a previously executed sentence of dishonorable or bad-conduct discharge is not imposed on a new trial, the Secretary concerned shall substitute therefor a form of discharge authorized for administrative issuance unless the accused is to serve out the remainder of his enlistment.

(c) If a previously executed sentence of dismissal is not imposed on a new trial, the Secretary concerned shall substitute therefor a form of discharge authorized for administrative issue, and the commissioned officer dismissed by that sentence may be reappointed by the President alone to such commissioned grade and with such rank as in the opinion of the President that former officer would have attained had he not been dismissed. The reappointment of such a former officer shall be without regard to the existence of a vacancy and shall affect the promotion status of other officers only insofar as the President may direct. All time between the dismissal and the reappointment shall be considered as actual service for all purposes, including the right to pay and allowances.

§ 876. Art. 76   Finality of proceedings, findings, and sentences

The appellate review of records of trial provided by this chapter, the proceedings, findings, and sentences of courts-martial as approved, reviewed, or affirmed as required by this chapter, and all dismissals and discharges carried into execution under sentences by courts-martial following approval, review, or affirmation as required by this chapter, are final and conclusive. Orders publishing the proceedings of courts-martial and all action taken pursuant to those proceedings are binding upon all departments, courts, agencies, and officers of the United States, subject only to action upon a petition for a new trial as provided in section 873 of this title (article 73) and to action by the Secretary concerned as provided in section 874 of this title (article 74), and the authority of the President.

§ 876a. Art. 76a   Leave required to be taken pending review of certain court-martial convictions

Under regulations prescribed by the Secretary concerned, an accused who has been sentenced by a court-martial may be required to take leave pending completion of action under this subchapter if the sentence, as approved under section 860 of this title (article 60), includes an unsuspended dismissal or an unsuspended dishonorable or bad-conduct discharge. The accused may be required to begin such leave on the date on which the sentence is approved under section 860 of this title (article 60) or at any time after such date, and such leave may be continued until the date on which action under this subchapter is completed or may be terminated at any earlier time.

§ 876b. Art. 76b   Lack of mental capacity or mental responsibility: commitment of accused for examination and treatment

(a) Persons incompetent to stand trial.

(1) In the case of a person determined under this chapter to be presently suffering from a mental disease or defect rendering the person mentally incompetent to the extent that the person is unable to understand the nature of the proceedings against that person or to conduct or cooperate intelligently in the defense of the case, the general court-martial convening authority for that person shall commit the person to the custody of the Attorney General.

(2) The Attorney General shall take action in accordance with section 4241(d) of title 18.

(3) If at the end of the period for hospitalization provided for in section 4241(d) of title 18, it is determined that the committed person's mental condition has not so improved as to permit the trial to proceed, action shall be taken in accordance with section 4246 of such title.

(4) (A) When the director of a facility in which a person is hospitalized pursuant to paragraph (2) determines that the person has recovered to such an extent that the person is able to understand the nature of the proceedings against the person and to conduct or cooperate intelligently in the defense of the case, the director shall promptly transmit a notification of that determination to the Attorney General and to the general court-martial convening authority for the person. The director shall send a copy of the notification to the person's counsel.

(B) Upon receipt of a notification, the general court-martial convening authority shall promptly take custody of the person unless the person covered by the notification is no longer subject to this chapter. If the person is no longer subject to this chapter, the Attorney General shall take any action within the authority of the Attorney General that the Attorney General considers appropriate regarding the person.

(C) The director of the facility may retain custody of the person for not more than 30 days after transmitting the notifications required by subparagraph (A).

(5) In the application of section 4246 of title 18 to a case under this subsection, references to the court that ordered the commitment of a person, and to the clerk of such court, shall be deemed to refer to the general court-martial convening authority for that person. However, if the person is no longer subject to this chapter at a time relevant to the application of such section to the person, the United States district court for the district where the person is hospitalized or otherwise may be found shall be considered as the court that ordered the commitment of the person.

(b) Persons found not guilty by reason of lack of mental responsibility.

(1) If a person is found by a court-martial not guilty only by reason of lack of mental responsibility, the person shall be committed to a suitable facility until the person is eligible for release in accordance with this section.

(2) The court-martial shall conduct a hearing on the mental condition in accordance with subsection (c) of section 4243 of title 18. Subsections (b) and (d) of that section shall apply with respect to the hearing.

(3) A report of the results of the hearing shall be made to the general court-martial convening authority for the person.

(4) If the court-martial fails to find by the standard specified in subsection (d) of section 4243 of title 18 that the person's release would not create a substantial risk of bodily injury to another person or serious damage of property of another due to a present mental disease or defect —

(A) the general court-martial convening authority may commit the person to the custody of the Attorney General; and

(B) the Attorney General shall take action in accordance with subsection (e) of section 4243 of title 18.

(5) Subsections (f), (g), and (h) of section 4243 of title 18 shall apply in the case of a person hospitalized pursuant to paragraph (4)(B), except that the United States district court for the district where the person is hospitalized shall be considered as the court that ordered the person's commitment.

(c) General provisions.

(1) Except as otherwise provided in this subsection and subsection (d)(1), the provisions of section 4247 of title 18 apply in the administration of this section.

(2) In the application of section 4247(d) of title 18 to hearings conducted by a court-martial under this section or by (or by order of) a general court-martial convening authority under this section, the reference in that section to section 3006A of such title does not apply.

(d) Applicability.

(1) The provisions of chapter 313 of title 18 referred to in this section apply according to the provisions of this section notwithstanding section 4247(j) of title 18.

(2) If the status of a person as described in section 802 of this title (article

2) terminates while the person is, pursuant to this section, in the custody of the Attorney General, hospitalized, or on conditional release under a prescribed regimen of medical, psychiatric, or psychological care or treatment, the provisions of this section establishing requirements and procedures regarding a person no longer subject to this chapter shall continue to apply to that person notwithstanding the change of status.

SUBCHAPTER X. PUNITIVE ARTICLES

§ 877. Art. 77   Principals

Any person punishable under this chapter who —

(1) commits an offense punishable by this chapter, or aids, abets, counsels, commands, or procures its commission; or

(2) causes an act to be done which if directly performed by him would be punishable by this chapter;

is a principal.

§ 878. Art. 78   Accessory after the fact

Any person subject to this chapter who, knowing that an offense punishable by this chapter has been committed, receives, comforts, or assists the offender in order to hinder or prevent his apprehension, trial, or punishment shall be punished as a court-martial may direct.

§ 879. Art. 79   Conviction of lesser offense

An accused may be found guilty of an offense necessarily included in the offense charged or of an attempt to commit either the offense charged or an offense necessarily included therein.

§ 880. Art. 80   Attempts

(a) An act, done with specific intent to commit an offense under this chapter, amounting to more than mere preparation and tending, even though failing, to effect its commission, is an attempt to commit that offense.

(b) Any person subject to this chapter who attempts to commit any offense punishable by this chapter shall be punished as a court-martial may direct, unless otherwise specifically prescribed.

(c) Any person subject to this chapter may be convicted of an attempt to commit an offense although it appears on the trial that the offense was consummated.

§ 881. Art. 81   Conspiracy

(a) Any person subject to this chapter who conspires with any other person to commit an offense under this chapter shall, if one or more of the conspirators does an act to effect the object of the conspiracy, be punished as a court-martial may direct.

(b) Any person subject to this chapter who conspires with any other person to commit an offense under the law of war, and who knowingly does an overt act to effect the object of the conspiracy, shall be punished, if death results to one or more of the victims, by death or such other punishment as a court-martial or military commission may direct, and, if death does not result to any of the victims, by such punishment, other than death, as a court-martial or military commission may direct.

§ 882. Art. 82   Solicitation

(a) Any person subject to this chapter who solicits or advises another or others to desert in violation of section 885 of this title (article 85) or mutiny in violation of section 894 of this title (article 94) shall, if the offense solicited or advised is attempted or committed, be punished with the punishment provided for the commission of the offense, but, if the offense solicited or advised is not committed or attempted, he shall be punished as a court-martial may direct.

(b) Any person subject to this chapter who solicits or advises another or others to commit an act of misbehavior before the enemy in violation of section 899 of this title (article 99) or sedition in violation of section 894 of this title (article 94) shall, if the offense solicited or advised is committed, be punished with the punishment provided for the commission of the offense, but, if the offense solicited or advised is not committed, he shall be punished as a court-martial may direct.

§ 883. Art. 83   Fraudulent enlistment, appointment, or separation

Any person who —

(1) procures his own enlistment or appointment in the armed forces by knowingly false representation or deliberate concealment as to his qualifications for that enlistment or appointment and receives pay or allowances thereunder; or

(2) procures his own separation from the armed forces by knowingly false representation or deliberate concealment as to his eligibility for that separation;

shall be punished as a court-martial may direct.

§ 884. Art. 84   Unlawful enlistment, appointment, or separation

Any person subject to this chapter who effects an enlistment or appointment in or a separation from the armed forces of any person who is known to him to be ineligible for that enlistment, appointment, or separation because it is prohibited by law, regulation, or order shall be punished as a court-martial may direct.

§ 885. Art. 85   Desertion

(a) Any member of the armed forces who —

(1) without authority goes or remains absent from his unit, organization, or place of duty with intent to remain away therefrom permanently;

(2) quits his unit, organization, or place of duty with intent to avoid

hazardous duty or to shirk important service; or

(3) without being regularly separated from one of the armed forces enlists or accepts an appointment in the same or another one of the armed forces without fully disclosing the fact that he has not been regularly separated, or enters any foreign armed service except when authorized by the United States;

is guilty of desertion.

(b) Any commissioned officer of the armed forces who, after tender of his resignation and before notice of its acceptance, quits his post or proper duties without leave and with intent to remain away therefrom permanently is guilty of desertion.

(c) Any person found guilty of desertion or attempt to desert shall be punished, if the offense is committed in time of war, by death or such other punishment as a court-martial may direct, but if the desertion or attempt to desert occurs at any other time, by such punishment, other than death, as a court-martial may direct.

§ 886. Art. 86   Absence without leave

Any member of the armed forces who, without authority —

(1) fails to go to his appointed place of duty at the time prescribed;

(2) goes from that place; or

(3) absents himself or remains absent from his unit, organization, or place of duty at which he is required to be at the time prescribed;

shall be punished as a court-martial may direct.

§ 887. Art. 87   Missing movement

Any person subject to this chapter who through neglect or design misses the movement of a ship, aircraft, or unit with which he is required in the course of duty to move shall be punished as a court-martial may direct.

§ 888. Art. 88   Contempt toward officials

Any commissioned officer who uses contemptuous words against the President, the Vice President, Congress, the Secretary of Defense, the Secretary of a military department, the Secretary of Homeland Security, or the Governor or legislature of any State, Commonwealth, or possession in which he is on duty or present shall be punished as a court-martial may direct.

§ 889. Art. 89   Disrespect toward superior commissioned officer

Any person subject to this chapter who behaves with disrespect toward his superior commissioned officer shall be punished as a court-martial may direct.

§ 890. Art. 90   Assaulting or willfully disobeying superior commissioned officer

Any person subject to this chapter who —

(1) strikes his superior commissioned officer or draws or lifts up any weapon

or offers any violence against him while he is in the execution of his office; or

(2) willfully disobeys a lawful command of his superior commissioned officer;

shall be punished, if the offense is committed in time of war, by death or such other punishment as a court-martial may direct, and if the offense is committed at any other time, by such punishment, other than death, as a court-martial may direct.

§ 891. Art. 91   Insubordinate conduct toward warrant officer, noncommissioned officer, or petty officer

Any warrant officer or enlisted member who —

(1) strikes or assaults a warrant officer, noncommissioned officer, or petty officer, while that officer is in the execution of his office;

(2) willfully disobeys the lawful order of a warrant officer, noncommissioned officer, or petty officer; or

(3) treats with contempt or is disrespectful in language or deportment toward a warrant officer, noncommissioned officer, or petty officer, while that officer is in the execution of his office;

shall be punished as a court-martial may direct.

§ 892. Art. 92   Failure to obey order or regulation

Any person subject to this chapter who —

(1) violates or fails to obey any lawful general order or regulation;

(2) having knowledge of any other lawful order issued by a member of the armed forces, which it is his duty to obey, fails to obey the order; or

(3) is derelict in the performance of his duties;

shall be punished as a court-martial may direct.

§ 893. Art. 93   Cruelty and maltreatment

Any person subject to this chapter who is guilty of cruelty toward, or oppression or maltreatment of, any person subject to his orders shall be punished as a court-martial may direct.

§ 894. Art. 94   Mutiny or sedition

(a) Any person subject to this chapter who —

(1) with intent to usurp or override lawful military authority, refuses, in concert with any other person, to obey orders or otherwise do his duty or creates any violence or disturbance is guilty of mutiny;

(2) with intent to cause the overthrow or destruction of lawful civil authority, creates, in concert with any other person, revolt, violence, or other disturbance against that authority is guilty of sedition;

(3) fails to do his utmost to prevent and suppress a mutiny or sedition being committed in his presence, or fails to take all reasonable means to inform his superior commissioned officer or commanding officer of a mutiny or sedition

which he knows or has reason to believe is taking place, is guilty of a failure to suppress or report a mutiny or sedition.

(b) A person who is found guilty of attempted mutiny, mutiny, sedition, or failure to suppress or report a mutiny or sedition shall be punished by death or such other punishment as a court-martial may direct.

§ 895. Art. 95   Resistance, flight, breach of arrest, and escape

Any person subject to this chapter who —

(1) resists apprehension;

(2) flees from apprehension;

(3) breaks arrest; or

(4) escapes from custody or confinement;

shall be punished as a court-martial may direct.

§ 896. Art. 96   Releasing prisoner without proper authority

Any person subject to this chapter who, without proper authority, releases any prisoner committed to his charge, or who through neglect or design suffers any such prisoner to escape, shall be punished as a court-martial may direct, whether or not the prisoner was committed in strict compliance with law.

§ 897. Art. 97   Unlawful detention

Any person subject to this chapter who, except as provided by law, apprehends, arrests, or confines any person shall be punished as a court-martial may direct.

§ 898. Art. 98   Noncompliance with procedural rules

Any person subject to this chapter who —

(1) is responsible for unnecessary delay in the disposition of any case of a person accused of an offense under this chapter; or

(2) knowingly and intentionally fails to enforce or comply with any provision of this chapter regulating the proceedings before, during, or after trial of an accused;

shall be punished as a court-martial may direct.

§ 899. Art. 99   Misbehavior before the enemy

Any member of the armed forces who before or in the presence of the enemy —

(1) runs away;

(2) shamefully abandons, surrenders, or delivers up any command, unit, place, or military property which it is his duty to defend;

(3) through disobedience, neglect, or intentional misconduct endangers the safety of any such command, unit, place, or military property;

(4) casts away his arms or ammunition;

(5) is guilty of cowardly conduct;

(6) quits his place of duty to plunder or pillage;

(7) causes false alarms in any command, unit, or place under control of the armed forces;

(8) willfully fails to do his utmost to encounter, engage, capture, or destroy any enemy troops, combatants, vessels, aircraft, or any other thing, which it is his duty so to encounter, engage, capture, or destroy; or

(9) does not afford all practicable relief and assistance to any troops, combatants, vessels, or aircraft of the armed forces belonging to the United States or their allies when engaged in battle;

shall be punished by death or such other punishment as a court-martial may direct.

§ 900. Art. 100   Subordinate compelling surrender

Any person subject to this chapter who compels or attempts to compel the commander of any place, vessel, aircraft, or other military property, or of any body of members of the armed forces, to give it up to an enemy or to abandon it, or who strikes the colors or flag to an enemy without proper authority, shall be punished by death or such other punishment as a court-martial may direct.

§ 901. Art. 101   Improper use of countersign

Any person subject to this chapter who in time of war discloses the parole or countersign to any person not entitled to receive it or who gives to another who is entitled to receive and use the parole or countersign a different parole or countersign from that which, to his knowledge, he was authorized and required to give, shall be punished by death or such other punishment as a court-martial may direct.

§ 902. Art. 102   Forcing a safeguard

Any person subject to this chapter who forces a safeguard shall suffer death or such other punishment as a court-martial may direct.

§ 903. Art. 103   Captured or abandoned property

(a) All persons subject to this chapter shall secure all public property taken from the enemy for the service of the United States, and shall give notice and turn over to the proper authority without delay all captured or abandoned property in their possession, custody, or control.

(b) Any person subject to this chapter who —

(1) fails to carry out the duties prescribed in subsection (a);

(2) buys, sells, trades, or in any way deals in or disposes of captured or abandoned property, whereby he receives or expects any profit, benefit, or advantage to himself or another directly or indirectly connected with himself; or

(3) engages in looting or pillaging;

shall be punished as a court-martial may direct.

§ 904. Art. 104 Aiding the enemy

Any person who —

(1) aids, or attempts to aid, the enemy with arms, ammunition, supplies, money, or other things; or

(2) without proper authority, knowingly harbors or protects or gives intelligence to, or communicates or corresponds with or holds any intercourse with the enemy, either directly or indirectly;

shall suffer death or such other punishment as a court-martial or military commission may direct. This section does not apply to a military commission established under chapter 47A of this title.

§ 905. Art. 105 Misconduct as prisoner

Any person subject to this chapter who, while in the hands of the enemy in time of war —

(1) for the purpose of securing favorable treatment by his captors acts without proper authority in a manner contrary to law, custom, or regulation, to the detriment of others of whatever nationality held by the enemy as civilian or military prisoners; or

(2) while in a position of authority over such persons maltreats them without justifiable cause;

shall be punished as a court-martial may direct.

§ 906. Art. 106 Spies

Any person who in time of war is found lurking as a spy or acting as a spy in or about any place, vessel, or aircraft, within the control or jurisdiction of any of the armed forces, or in or about any shipyard, any manufacturing or industrial plant, or any other place or institution engaged in work in aid of the prosecution of the war by the United States, or elsewhere, shall be tried by a general court-martial or by a military commission and on conviction shall be punished by death. This section does not apply to a military commission established under chapter 47A of this title.

§ 906a. Art. 106a Espionage

(a) (1) Any person subject to this chapter who, with intent or reason to believe that it is to be used to the injury of the United States or to the advantage of a foreign nation, communicates, delivers, or transmits, or attempts to communicate, deliver, or transmit, to any entity described in paragraph (2), either directly or indirectly, anything described in paragraph (3) shall be punished as a court-martial may direct, except that if the accused is found guilty of an offense that directly concerns (A) nuclear weaponry, military spacecraft or satellites, early warning systems, or other means of defense or retaliation against large scale attack, (B) war plans, (C) communications intelligence or cryptographic information, or (D) any other major weapons system or major element of defense strategy, the accused shall be punished by death or such other punishment as a court-martial may direct.

(2) An entity referred to in paragraph (1) is —

(A) a foreign government;

(B) a faction or party or military or naval force within a foreign country, whether recognized or unrecognized by the United States; or

(C) a representative, officer, agent, employee, subject, or citizen of such a government, faction, party, or force.

(3) A thing referred to in paragraph (1) is a document, writing, code book, signal book, sketch, photograph, photographic negative, blueprint, plan, map, model, note, instrument, appliance, or information relating to the national defense.

(b) (1) No person may be sentenced by court-martial to suffer death for an offense under this section (article) unless —

(A) the members of the court-martial unanimously find at least one of the aggravating factors set out in subsection (c); and

(B) the members unanimously determine that any extenuating or mitigating circumstances are substantially outweighed by any aggravating circumstances, including the aggravating factors set out in subsection (c).

(2) Findings under this subsection may be based on —

(A) evidence introduced on the issue of guilt or innocence;

(B) evidence introduced during the sentencing proceeding; or

(C) all such evidence.

(3) The accused shall be given broad latitude to present matters in extenuation and mitigation.

(c) A sentence of death may be adjudged by a court-martial for an offense under this section (article) only if the members unanimously find, beyond a reasonable doubt, one or more of the following aggravating factors:

(1) The accused has been convicted of another offense involving espionage or treason for which either a sentence of death or imprisonment for life was authorized by statute.

(2) In the commission of the offense, the accused knowingly created a grave risk of substantial damage to the national security.

(3) In the commission of the offense, the accused knowingly created a grave risk of death to another person.

(4) Any other factor that may be prescribed by the President by regulations under section 836 of this title (article 36)

§ 907. Art. 107   False official statements

Any person subject to this chapter who, with intent to deceive, signs any false record, return, regulation, order, or other official document, knowing it to be false, or makes any other false official statement knowing it to be false, shall be punished as a court-martial may direct.

§ 908. Art. 108   Military property of the United States – Loss, damage, destruction, or wrongful disposition

Any person subject to this chapter who, without proper authority –

(1) sells or otherwise disposes of;

(2) willfully or through neglect damages, destroys, or loses; or

(3) willfully or through neglect suffers to be lost, damaged, destroyed, sold, or wrongfully disposed of;

any military property of the United States, shall be punished as a court-martial may direct.

§ 909. Art. 109   Property other than military property of the United States – Waste, spoilage, or destruction

Any person subject to this chapter who willfully or recklessly wastes, spoils, or otherwise willfully and wrongfully destroys or damages any property other than military property of the United States shall be punished as a court-martial may direct.

§ 910. Art. 110   Improper hazarding of vessel

(a) Any person subject to this chapter who willfully and wrongfully hazards or suffers to be hazarded any vessel of the armed forces shall suffer death or such other punishment as a court-martial may direct.

(b) Any person subject to this chapter who negligently hazards or suffers to be hazarded any vessel of the armed forces shall be punished as a court-martial may direct.

§ 911. Art. 111   Drunken or reckless operation of a vehicle, aircraft, or vessel

(a) Any person subject to this chapter who —

(1) operates or physically controls any vehicle, aircraft, or vessel in a reckless or wanton manner or while impaired by a substance described in section 912a(b) of this title (article 112a(b)), or

(2) operates or is in actual physical control of any vehicle, aircraft, or vessel while drunk or when the alcohol concentration in the person's blood or breath is equal to or exceeds the applicable limit under subsection (b),

shall be punished as a court-martial may direct.

(b) (1) For purposes of subsection (a), the applicable limit on the alcohol concentration in a person's blood or breath is as follows:

(A) In the case of the operation or control of a vehicle, aircraft, or vessel in the United States, such limit is the lesser of —

(i) the blood alcohol content limit under the law of the State in which the conduct occurred, except as may be provided under paragraph (2) for conduct on a military installation that is in more than one State; or

(ii) the blood alcohol content limit specified in paragraph (3).

(B) In the case of the operation or control of a vehicle, aircraft, or vessel outside the United States, the applicable blood alcohol content limit is the blood alcohol content limit specified in paragraph (3) or such lower limit as the Secretary of Defense may by regulation prescribe.

(2) In the case of a military installation that is in more than one State, if those States have different blood alcohol content limits under their respective State laws, the Secretary may select one such blood alcohol content limit to apply uniformly on that installation.

(3) For purposes of paragraph (1), the blood alcohol content limit with respect to alcohol concentration in a person's blood is 0.10 grams of alcohol per 100 milliliters of blood and with respect to alcohol concentration in a person's breath is 0.10 grams of alcohol per 210 liters of breath, as shown by chemical analysis.

(4) In this subsection:

(A) The term "blood alcohol content limit" means the amount of alcohol concentration in a person's blood or breath at which operation or control of a vehicle, aircraft, or vessel is prohibited.

(B) The term "United States" includes the District of Columbia, the Commonwealth of Puerto Rico, the Virgin Islands, Guam, and American Samoa and the term "State" includes each of those jurisdictions.

§ 912. Art. 112   Drunk on duty

Any person subject to this chapter other than a sentinel or lookout, who is found drunk on duty, shall be punished as a court-martial may direct.

§ 912a. Art. 112a   Wrongful use, possession, etc., of controlled substances

(a) Any person subject to this chapter who wrongfully uses, possesses, manufactures, distributes, imports into the customs territory of the United States, exports from the United States, or introduces into an installation, vessel, vehicle, or aircraft used by or under the control of the armed forces a substance described in subsection (b) shall be punished as a court-martial may direct.

(b) The substances referred to in subsection (a) are the following:

(1) Opium, heroin, cocaine, amphetamine, lysergic acid diethylamide, methamphetamine, phencyclidine, barbituric acid, and marijuana and any compound or derivative of any such substance.

(2) Any substance not specified in clause (1) that is listed on a schedule of controlled substances prescribed by the President for the purposes of this article.

(3) Any other substance not specified in clause (1) or contained on a list prescribed by the President under clause (2) that is listed in schedules I through V of section 202 of the Controlled Substances Act.

§ 913. Art. 113   Misbehavior of sentinel

Any sentinel or look-out who is found drunk or sleeping upon his post, or leaves it before he is regularly relieved, shall be punished, if the offense is committed in time of war, by death or such other punishment as a court-martial may direct, but if the offense is committed at any other time, by such punishment other than death as a court-martial may direct.

§ 914. Art. 114   Dueling

Any person subject to this chapter who fights or promotes, or is concerned in or connives at fighting a duel, or who, having knowledge of a challenge sent or about to be sent, fails to report the fact promptly to the proper authority, shall be punished as a court-martial may direct.

§ 915. Art. 115   Malingering

Any person subject to this chapter who for the purpose of avoiding work, duty, or service —

(1) feigns illness, physical disablement, mental lapse or derangement; or

(2) intentionally inflicts self-injury;

shall be punished as a court-martial may direct.

§ 916. Art. 116   Riot or breach of peace

Any person subject to this chapter who causes or participates in any riot or breach of the peace shall be punished as a court-martial may direct.

§ 917. Art. 117   Provoking speeches or gestures

Any person subject to this chapter who uses provoking or reproachful words or gestures towards any other person subject to this chapter shall be punished as a court-martial may direct.

§ 918. Art. 118   Murder

Any person subject to this chapter who, without justification or excuse, unlawfully kills a human being, when he —

(1) has a premeditated design to kill;

(2) intends to kill or inflict great bodily harm;

(3) is engaged in an act which is inherently dangerous to another and evinces a wanton disregard of human life; or

(4) is engaged in the perpetration or attempted perpetration of burglary, sodomy, rape, rape of a child, sexual assault, sexual assault of a child, aggravated sexual contact, sexual abuse of a child, robbery, or aggravated arson;

is guilty of murder, and shall suffer such punishment as a court-martial may direct, except that if found guilty under clause (1) or (4), he shall suffer death or imprisonment for life as a court-martial may direct.

§ 919. Art. 119   Manslaughter

(a) Any person subject to this chapter who, with an intent to kill or inflict great bodily harm, unlawfully kills a human being in the heat of sudden passion caused by adequate provocation is guilty of voluntary manslaughter and shall be punished as a court-martial may direct.

(b) Any person subject to this chapter who, without an intent to kill or inflict great bodily harm, unlawfully kills a human being —

(1) by culpable negligence; or

(2) while perpetrating or attempting to perpetrate an offense, other than those named in clause (4) of section 918 of this title (article 118), directly affecting the person;

is guilty of involuntary manslaughter and shall be punished as a court-martial may direct.

§ 919a. Art. 119a   Death or injury of an unborn child

(a) (1) Any person subject to this chapter who engages in conduct that violates any of the provisions of law listed in subsection (b) and thereby causes the death of, or bodily injury (as defined in section 1365 of title 18) to, a child, who is in utero at the time the conduct takes place, is guilty of a separate offense under this section and shall, upon conviction, be punished by such punishment, other than death, as a court-martial may direct, which shall be consistent with the punishments prescribed by the President for that conduct had that injury or death occurred to the unborn child's mother.

(2) An offense under this section does not require proof that —

(i) the person engaging in the conduct had knowledge or should have had knowledge that the victim of the underlying offense was pregnant; or

(ii) the accused intended to cause the death of, or bodily injury to, the unborn child.

(3) If the person engaging in the conduct thereby intentionally kills or attempts to kill the unborn child, that person shall, instead of being punished under paragraph (1), be punished as provided under sections 880, 918, and 919(a) of this title (articles 80, 118, and 119(a)) for intentionally killing or attempting to kill a human being.

(4) Notwithstanding any other provision of law, the death penalty shall not be imposed for an offense under this section.

(b) The provisions referred to in subsection (a) are sections 918, 919(a), 919(b)(2), 920(a), 922, 924, 926, and 928 of this title (articles 118, 119(a), 119(b)(2), 120(a), 122, 124, 126, and 128).

(c) Nothing in this section shall be construed to permit the prosecution —

(1) of any person for conduct relating to an abortion for which the consent of the pregnant woman, or a person authorized by law to act on her behalf, has been obtained or for which such consent is implied by law;

(2) of any person for any medical treatment of the pregnant woman or her unborn child; or

(3) of any woman with respect to her unborn child.

(d) In this section, the term "unborn child" means a child in utero, and the term "child in utero" or "child, who is in utero" means a member of the species homo sapiens, at any stage of development, who is carried in the womb.

§ 920. Art. 120   Rape and sexual assault generally

(a) Rape. Any person subject to this chapter who commits a sexual act upon another person by —

(1) using unlawful force against that other person;

(2) using force causing or likely to cause death or grievous bodily harm to any person;

(3) threatening or placing that other person in fear that any person will be subjected to death, grievous bodily harm, or kidnapping;

(4) first rendering that other person unconscious; or

(5) administering to that other person by force or threat of force, or without the knowledge or consent of that person, a drug, intoxicant, or other similar substance and thereby substantially impairing the ability of that other person to appraise or control conduct;

is guilty of rape and shall be punished as a court-martial may direct.

(b) Sexual assault. Any person subject to this chapter who —

(1) commits a sexual act upon another person by —

(A) threatening or placing that other person in fear;

(B) causing bodily harm to that other person; or

(C) making a fraudulent representation that the sexual act serves a professional purpose; or

(D) inducing a belief by any artifice, pretense, or concealment that the person is another person;

(2) commits a sexual act upon another person when the person knows or reasonably should know that the other person is asleep, unconscious, or otherwise unaware that the sexual act is occurring; or

(3) commits a sexual act upon another person when the other person is incapable of consenting to the sexual act due to —

(A) impairment by any drug, intoxicant, or other similar substance, and that condition is known or reasonably should be known by the person; or

(B) a mental disease or defect, or physical disability, and that condition is known or reasonably should be known by the person;

is guilty of sexual assault and shall be punished as a court-martial may direct.

(c) Aggravated sexual contact. Any person subject to this chapter who commits or causes sexual contact upon or by another person, if to do so would violate subsection (a)(rape) had the sexual contact been a sexual act, is guilty of aggravated sexual contact and shall be punished as a court-martial may direct.

(d) Abusive sexual contact. Any person subject to this chapter who commits or causes sexual contact upon or by another person, if to do so would violate subsection (b) (aggravated sexual assault) had the sexual contact been a sexual act, is guilty of abusive sexual contact and shall be punished as a court-martial may direct.

(e) Proof of threat. In a prosecution under this section, in proving that a person made a threat, it need not be proven that the person actually intended to carry out the threat or had the ability to carry out the threat.

(f) Defenses — An accused may raise any applicable defenses available under this chapter or the Rules for Court-Martial. Marriage is not a defense for any conduct in issue in any prosecution under this section.

(g) Definitions. In this section:

(1) Sexual act. The term "sexual act" means —

(A) contact between the penis and the vulva or anus or mouth, and for purposes of this subparagraph contact involving the penis occurs upon penetration, however slight; or

(B) the penetration, however slight, of the vulva or anus or mouth of another by any part of the body or by any object, with an intent to abuse, humiliate, harass, or degrade any person or to arouse or gratify the sexual desire of any person.

(2) Sexual contact. The term "sexual contact" means —

(A) touching, or causing another person to touch, either directly or through the clothing, the genitalia, anus, groin, breast, inner thigh, or buttocks of any person, with an intent to abuse, humiliate, or degrade any person; or

(B) any touching, or causing another person to touch, either directly or through the clothing, any body part of any person, if done with an intent to arouse or gratify the sexual desires of any person.

Touching may be accomplished by any part of the body.

(3) Bodily harm. The term "bodily harm" means any offensive touching of another, however slight, including any nonconsensual sexual act or nonconsensual sexual contact.

(4) Grievous bodily harm. The term "grievous bodily harm" means serious

bodily injury. It includes fractured or dislocated bones, deep cuts, torn members of the body, serious damage to internal organs, and other severe bodily injuries. It does not include minor injuries such as a black eye or a bloody nose.

(5) Force. The term "force" means —

(A) the use of a weapon;

(B) the use of such physical strength or violence as is sufficient to overcome, restrain, or injure a person; or

(C) inflicting physical harm sufficient to coerce or compel submission by the victim.

(6) Unlawful force. The term "unlawful force" means an act of force done without legal justification or excuse.

(7) Threatening or placing that other person in fear. The term "threatening or placing that other person in fear" means a communication or action that is of sufficient consequence to cause a reasonable fear that non-compliance will result in the victim or another person being subjected to the wrongful action contemplated by the communication or action.

(8) Consent.

(A) The term "consent" means a freely given agreement to the conduct at issue by a competent person. An expression of lack of consent through words or conduct means there is no consent. Lack of verbal or physical resistance or submission resulting from use of force, threat of force, or placing another person in fear does not constitute consent. A current or previous dating or social or sexual relationship by itself or the manner of dress of the person involved with the accused in the conduct at issue shall not constitute consent.

(B) A sleeping, unconscious, or incompetent person cannot consent. A person cannot consent to force causing or likely to cause death or grievous bodily harm or to being rendered unconscious. A person cannot consent while under threat or in fear or under the circumstances described in subparagraph (C) or (D) of subsection (b)(1).

(C) Lack of consent may be inferred based on the circumstances of the offense. All the surrounding circumstances are to be considered in determining whether a person gave consent, or whether a person did not resist or ceased to resist only because of another person's actions.

§ 920a. Art. 120a   Stalking

(a) Any person subject to this section —

(1) who wrongfully engages in a course of conduct directed at a specific person that would cause a reasonable person to fear death or bodily harm, including sexual assault, to himself or herself or a member of his or her immediate family;

(2) who has knowledge, or should have knowledge, that the specific person will be placed in reasonable fear of death or bodily harm, including sexual assault, to himself or herself or a member of his or her immediate family; and

(3) whose acts induce reasonable fear in the specific person of death or bodily harm, including sexual assault, to himself or herself or to a member of his or her immediate family; is guilty of stalking and shall be punished as a court-martial may direct.

(b) In this section:

(1) The term "course of conduct" means —

(A) a repeated maintenance of visual or physical proximity to a specific person; or

(B) a repeated conveyance of verbal threat, written threats, or threats implied by conduct, or a combination of such threats, directed at or toward a specific person.

(2) The term "repeated", with respect to conduct, means two or more occasions of such conduct.

(3) The term "immediate family", in the case of a specific person, means a spouse, parent, child, or sibling of the person, or any other family member, relative, or intimate partner of the person who regularly resides in the household of the person or who within the six months preceding the commencement of the course of conduct regularly resided in the household of the person.

§ 920b. Art. 120b   Rape and Sexual Assault of a Child

(a) Rape of a child. Any person subject to this chapter who —

(1) commits a sexual act upon a child who has not attained the age of 12 years; or

(2) commits a sexual act upon a child who has attained the act of 12 years by —

(A) using force against any person;

(B) threatening or placing that child in fear;

(C) rendering that child unconscious; or

(D) administering to that child a drug, intoxicant, or other similar substance;

is guilty of rape of a child an shall be punished as a court-martial may direct.

(b) Sexual Assault of a Child. Any person subject to this chapter who commits a sexual act upon a child who has attained the age of 12 years is guilty of sexual assault of a child and shall be punished as a court-martial may direct.

(c) Sexual Abuse of a Child. Any person subject to this chapter who commits a lewd act upon a child is guilty of sexual abuse of a child and shall be punished as a court-martial may direct.

(d) Age of a Child.

(1) Under 12 years. In a prosecution under this section, it need not be proven that the accused knew the age of the other person engaging in the sexual act or lewd act. It is not a defense that the accused reasonably believed that the child had attained the age of 12 years.

(2) Under 16 years. In a prosecution under this section, it need not be proven that the accused knew that the other person engaging in the sexual act or lewd act had not attained the age of 16 years, but it is a defense in a prosecution under subsection (b) (sexual assault of a child) or subsection (c) (sexual abuse of a child), which the accused must prove by a preponderance of the evidence, that the accused reasonably believed that the child had attained the age of 16 years, if the child had in fact attained at least the age of 12 years.

(e) Proof of Threat. In a prosecution under this section, in proving that a person made a threat, it need not be proven that the person actually intended to carry out the threat or had the ability to carry out the threat.

(f) Marriage. In a prosecution under subsection (b) (sexual assault on a child) or subsection (c) (sexual abuse of a child), it is a defense, which the accused must prove by a preponderance of the evidence, that the persons engaging in the sexual act or lewd act were at that time married to each other, except where the accused commits a sexual act upon the person when the accused knows or reasonably should know that the other person is asleep, unconscious, or otherwise unaware that the sexual act is occurring or when the other person is incapable of consenting to the sexual act due to impairment by any drug, intoxicant, or other similar substance, and that condition was known or reasonably should have been known by the accused.

(g) Consent. Lack of consent is not an element and need not be proven in any prosecution under this section. A child not legally married to the person committing the sexual act, lewd act, or use of force cannot consent to any sexual act, lewd act, or use of force.

(h) Definitions. In this section:

(1) Sexual act and sexual contact. The terms "sexual act" and "sexual contact" have the meanings given those terms in section 920(g) of this article (article 120(g)).

(2) Force. The term "force" means —

(A) the use of a weapon;

(B) the use of such physical strength or violence as is sufficient to overcome, restrain, or injure a child; or

(C) inflicting physical harm.

In the case of a parent-child or similar relationship, the use or abuse of parental or similar authority is sufficient to constitute the use of force.

(3) Threatening or placing that child in fear. The term "threatening or placing that child in fear" means a communication or action that is of sufficient consequence to cause the child to fear that non-compliance will result in the child or another person being subjected to the action contemplated by the communication or action.

(4) Child. The term "child" means any person who as not attained the age of 16 years.

(5) Lewd act. The term "lewd act" means —

(A) any sexual contact with a child;

(B) intentionally exposing one's genitalia, anus, buttocks, or female areola or nipple to a child by any means, including via any communication technology, with an intent to abuse, humiliate, or degrade any person, or to arouse or gratify the sexual desire of any person;

(C) intentionally communicating indecent language to a child by any means, including via any communication technology, with an intent to abuse, humiliate, or degrade any person, or to arouse or gratify the sexual desire of any person; or

(D) any indecent conduct, intentionally done with or in the presence of a child, including via any communication technology, that amounts to a form of immorality relating to sexual impurity which is grossly vulgar, obscene, and repugnant to common propriety, and tends to incite sexual desire or deprave morals with respect to sexual relations.

§ 920c. Art. 120c   Other Sexual Misconduct

(a) Indecent Viewing, Visual Recording, or Broadcasting. Any person subject to this chapter who, without legal justification or lawful authorization —

(1) knowingly and wrongfully views the private area of another person, without that person's consent and under circumstances in which that other person has a reasonably expectation of privacy;

(2) knowingly photographs, videotapes, films, or records by any means the private area of another person, without that other person's consent and under circumstances in which that other person has a reasonable expectation of privacy;

(3) knowingly broadcasts or distributes any such recording that the person knew or reasonably should have known was made under the circumstances proscribed in paragraphs (1) and (2);

is guitly of an offense under this section and shall be punished as a court-martial may direct.

(b) Forcible Pandering. Any person subject to this chapter who compels another person to engage in an act of prostitution with any person is guilty of forcible pandering and shall be punished as a court-martial may direct.

(c) Indecent Exposure. Any person subject to this chapter who intentionally exposes, in an indecent manner, the genitalia, anus, buttocks, or female areola or nipple is guilty of indecent exposure and shall be punished as a court-martial may direct.

(d) Definitions — In this section:

(1) Act of prostitution. The term "act of prostitution" means a sexual act or sexual contact (as defined in section 920(g) of this title (article 120(g))) on account of which anything of value is given to, or received by, any person.

(2) Private area. The term "private area" means the naked or underwear-clad genitalia, anus, buttocks, or female areola or nipple.

(3) Reasonable expectation of privacy. The term "under circumstances in which that other person has a reasonable expectation of privacy" means —

(A) circumstances in which a reasonable person would believe that he or she could disrobe in privacy, without being concerned that an image of a private area of the person was being captured; or

(B) circumstances in which a reasonable person would believe that a private area of the person would not be visible to the public.

(4) Broadcast. The term "broadcast" means to electronically transmit a visual image with the intent that it be viewed by a person or persons.

(5) Distribute. The term "distribute" means delivering to the actual or constructive possession of another, including transmission by electronic means.

(6) Indecent manner. The term "indecent manner" means conduct that amounts to a form of immorality relating to sexual impurity which is grossly vulgar, obscene, and repugnant to common propriety, and tends to excite sexual desire or deprave morals with respect to sexual relations.

§ 921. Art. 121   Larceny and wrongful appropriation

(a) Any person subject to this chapter who wrongfully takes, obtains, or withholds, by any means, from the possession of the owner or of any other person any money, personal property, or article of value of any kind —

(1) with intent permanently to deprive or defraud another person of the use and benefit of property or to appropriate it to his own use or the use of any person other than the owner, steals that property and is guilty of larceny; or

(2) with intent temporarily to deprive or defraud another person of the use and benefit of property or to appropriate it to his own use or the use of any person other than the owner, is guilty of wrongful appropriation.

(b) Any person found guilty of larceny or wrongful appropriation shall be punished as a court-martial may direct.

§ 922. Art. 122   Robbery

Any person subject to this chapter who with intent to steal takes anything of value from the person or in the presence of another, against his will, by means of force or violence or fear of immediate or future injury to his person or property or to the person or property of a relative or member of his family or of anyone in his company at the time of the robbery, is guilty of robbery and shall be punished as a court-martial may direct.

§ 923. Art. 123   Forgery

Any person subject to this chapter who, with intent to defraud —

(1) falsely makes or alters any signature to, or any part of, any writing which would, if genuine, apparently impose a legal liability on another or change his legal right or liability to his prejudice; or

(2) utters, offers, issues, or transfers such a writing, known by him to be so made or altered;

is guilty of forgery and shall be punished as a court-martial may direct.

§ 923a. Art. 123a   Making, drawing, or uttering check, draft, or order without sufficient funds

Any person subject to this chapter who —

(1) for the procurement of any article or thing of value, with intent to defraud; or

(2) for the payment of any past due obligation, or for any other purpose, with intent to deceive;

makes, draws, utters, or delivers any check, draft, or order for the payment of money upon any bank or other depository, knowing at the time that the maker or drawer has not or will not have sufficient funds in, or credit with, the bank or other depository for the payment of that check, draft, or order in full upon its presentment, shall be punished as a court-martial may direct. The making, drawing, uttering, or delivering by a maker or drawer of a check, draft, or order, payment of which is refused by the drawee because of insufficient funds of the maker or drawer in the drawee's possession or control, is prima facie evidence of his intent to defraud or deceive and of his knowledge of insufficient funds in, or credit with, that bank or other depository, unless the maker or drawer pays the holder the amount due within five days after receiving notice, orally or in writing, that the check, draft, or order was not paid on presentment. In this section, the word "credit" means an arrangement or understanding, express or implied, with the bank or other depository for the payment of that check, draft, or order.

§ 924. Art. 124   Maiming

Any person subject to this chapter who, with intent to injure, disfigure, or disable, inflicts upon the person of another an injury which —

(1) seriously disfigures his person by any mutilation thereof;

(2) destroys or disables any member or organ of his body; or

(3) seriously diminishes his physical vigor by the injury of any member or organ;

is guilty of maiming and shall be punished as a court-martial may direct.

§ 925. Art. 125   Sodomy

(a) Any person subject to this chapter who engages in unnatural carnal copulation with another person of the same or opposite sex or with an animal is guilty of sodomy. Penetration, however slight, is sufficient to complete the offense.

(b) Any person found guilty of sodomy shall be punished as a court-martial may direct.

§ 926. Art. 126   Arson

(a) Any person subject to this chapter who willfully and maliciously burns or sets on fire an inhabited dwelling, or any other structure, movable or immovable, wherein to the knowledge of the offender there is at the time a human being, is guilty of aggravated arson and shall be punished as a court-martial may direct.

(b) Any person subject to this chapter who willfully and maliciously burns or sets fire to the property of another, except as provided in subsection (a), is guilty of simple arson and shall be punished as a court-martial may direct.

§ 927. Art. 127   Extortion

Any person subject to this chapter who communicates threats to another person with the intention thereby to obtain anything of value or any acquittance, advantage, or immunity is guilty of extortion and shall be punished as a court-martial may direct.

§ 928. Art. 128   Assault

(a) Any person subject to this chapter who attempts or offers with unlawful force or violence to do bodily harm to another person, whether or not the attempt or offer is consummated, is guilty of assault and shall be punished as a court-martial may direct.

(b) Any person subject to this chapter who —

(1) commits an assault with a dangerous weapon or other means or force likely to produce death or grievous bodily harm; or

(2) commits an assault and intentionally inflicts grievous bodily harm with or without a weapon;

is guilty of aggravated assault and shall be punished as a court-martial may direct.

§ 929. Art. 129   Burglary

Any person subject to this chapter who, with intent to commit an offense punishable under sections 918-928 of this title (articles 118-128), breaks and enters, in the nighttime, the dwelling house of another, is guilty of burglary and shall be punished as a court-martial may direct.

§ 930. Art. 130   Housebreaking

Any person subject to this chapter who unlawfully enters the building or structure of another with intent to commit a criminal offense therein is guilty of housebreaking and shall be punished as a court-martial may direct.

§ 931. Art. 131   Perjury

Any person subject to this chapter who in a judicial proceeding or in a course of justice willfully and corruptly —

(1) upon a lawful oath or in any form allowed by law to be substituted for an oath, gives any false testimony material to the issue or matter of inquiry; or

(2) in any declaration, certificate, verification, or statement under penalty of perjury as permitted under section 1746 of title 28, subscribes any false statement material to the issue or matter of inquiry;

is guilty of perjury and shall be punished as a court-martial may direct.

§ 932. Art. 132   Frauds against the United States

Any person subject to this chapter —

(1) who, knowing it to be false or fraudulent —

(A) makes any claim against the United States or any officer thereof; or

(B) presents to any person in the civil or military service thereof, for approval or payment, any claim against the United States or any officer thereof;

(2) who, for the purpose of obtaining the approval, allowance, or payment of any claim against the United States or any officer thereof —

(A) makes or uses any writing or other paper knowing it to contain any false or fraudulent statements;

(B) makes any oath to any fact or to any writing or other paper knowing the oath to be false; or

(C) forges or counterfeits any signature upon any writing or other paper, or uses any such signature knowing it to be forged or counterfeited;

(3) who, having charge, possession, custody, or control of any money, or other property of the United States, furnished or intended for the armed forces thereof, knowingly delivers to any person having authority to receive it, any amount thereof less than that for which he receives a certificate or receipt; or

(4) who, being authorized to make or deliver any paper certifying the receipt of any property of the United States furnished or intended for the armed forces thereof, makes or delivers to any person such writing without having full knowledge of the truth of the statements therein contained and with intent to defraud the United States;

shall, upon conviction, be punished as a court-martial may direct.

§ 933. Art. 133   Conduct unbecoming an officer and a gentleman

Any commissioned officer, cadet, or midshipman who is convicted of conduct unbecoming an officer and a gentleman shall be punished as a court-martial may direct.

§ 934. Art. 134   General article

Though not specifically mentioned in this chapter, all disorders and neglects to the prejudice of good order and discipline in the armed forces, all conduct of a nature to bring discredit upon the armed forces, and crimes and offenses not capital, of which persons subject to this chapter may be guilty, shall be taken cognizance of by a general, special, or summary court-martial, according to the nature and degree of the offense, and shall be punished at the discretion of that court.

SUBCHAPTER XI.   MISCELLANEOUS PROVISIONS

§ 935. Art. 135   Courts of inquiry

(a) Courts of inquiry to investigate any matter may be convened by any person authorized to convene a general court-martial or by any other person designated by the Secretary concerned for that purpose, whether or not the persons involved have requested such an inquiry.

(b) A court of inquiry consists of three or more commissioned officers. For each court of inquiry the convening authority shall also appoint counsel for the court.

(c) Any person subject to this chapter whose conduct is subject to inquiry shall be designated as a party. Any person subject to this chapter or employed by the Department of Defense who has a direct interest in the subject of inquiry has the right to be designated as a party upon request to the court. Any person designated as a party shall be given due notice and has the right to be present, to be represented by counsel, to cross-examine witnesses, and to introduce evidence.

(d) Members of a court of inquiry may be challenged by a party, but only for cause stated to the court.

(e) The members, counsel, the reporter, and interpreters of courts of inquiry shall take an oath to faithfully perform their duties.

(f) Witnesses may be summoned to appear and testify and be examined before courts of inquiry, as provided for courts-martial.

(g) Courts of inquiry shall make findings of fact but may not express opinions or make recommendations unless required to do so by the convening authority.

(h) Each court of inquiry shall keep a record of its proceedings, which shall be authenticated by the signatures of the president and counsel for the court and forwarded to the convening authority. If the record cannot be authenticated by the president, it shall be signed by a member in lieu of the president. If the record cannot be authenticated by the counsel for the court, it shall be signed by a member in lieu of the counsel.

§ 936. Art. 136   Authority to administer oaths and to act as notary

(a) The following persons on active duty or performing inactive-duty training may administer oaths for the purposes of military administration, including military justice:

(1) All judge advocates.

(2) All summary courts-martial.

(3) All adjutants, assistant adjutants, acting adjutants, and personnel adjutants.

(4) All commanding officers of the Navy, Marine Corps, and Coast Guard.

(5) All staff judge advocates and legal officers, and acting or assistant staff judge advocates and legal officers.

(6) All other persons designated by regulations of the armed forces or by statute.

(b) The following persons on active duty or performing inactive-duty training may administer oaths necessary in the performance of their duties:

(1) The president, military judge, trial counsel, and assistant trial counsel for all general and special courts-martial.

(2) The president and the counsel for the court of any court of inquiry.

(3) All officers designated to take a deposition.

(4) All persons detailed to conduct an investigation.

(5) All recruiting officers.

(6) All other persons designated by regulations of the armed forces or by statute.

(c) The judges of the United States Court of Appeals for the Armed Forces may administer the oaths authorized by subsections (a) and (b).

§ 937. Art. 137   Articles to be explained

(a) (1) The sections of this title (articles of the Uniform Code of Military Justice) specified in paragraph (3) shall be carefully explained to each enlisted member at the time of (or within fourteen days after) —

(A) the member's initial entrance on active duty; or

(B) the member's initial entrance into a duty status with a reserve component.

(2) Such sections (articles) shall be explained again —

(A) after the member has completed six months of active duty or, in the case of a member of a reserve component, after the member has completed basic or recruit training; and

(B) at the time when the member reenlists.

(3) This subsection applies with respect to sections 802, 803, 807-815, 825,

827, 831, 837, 838, 855, 877-934, and 937-939 of this title (articles 2, 3, 7-15, 25, 27, 31, 37, 38, 55, 77-134, and 137-139).

(b) The text of the Uniform Code of Military Justice and of the regulations prescribed by the President under such Code shall be made available to a member on active duty or to a member of a reserve component, upon request by the member, for the member's personal examination.

§ 938. Art. 138   Complaints of wrongs

Any member of the armed forces who believes himself wronged by his commanding officer, and who, upon due application to that commanding officer, is refused redress, may complain to any superior commissioned officer, who shall forward the complaint to the officer exercising general court-martial jurisdiction over the officer against whom it is made. The officer exercising general court-martial jurisdiction shall examine into the complaint and take proper measures for redressing the wrong complained of; and he shall, as soon as possible, send to the Secretary concerned a true statement of that complaint, with the proceedings had thereon.

§ 939. Art. 139   Redress of injuries to property

(a) Whenever complaint is made to any commanding officer that willful damage has been done to the property of any person or that his property has been wrongfully taken by members of the armed forces, he may, under such regulations as the Secretary concerned may prescribe, convene a board to investigate the complaint. The board shall consist of from one to three commissioned officers and, for the purpose of that investigation, it has power to summon witnesses and examine them upon oath, to receive depositions or other documentary evidence, and to assess the damages sustained against the responsible parties. The assessment of damages made by the board is subject to the approval of the commanding officer, and in the amount approved by him shall be charged against the pay of the offenders. The order of the commanding officer directing charges herein authorized is conclusive on any disbursing officer for the payment by him to the injured parties of the damages so assessed and approved.

(b) If the offenders cannot be ascertained, but the organization or detachment to which they belong is known, charges totaling the amount of damages assessed and approved may be made in such proportion as may be considered just upon the individual members thereof who are shown to have been present at the scene at the time the damages complained of were inflicted, as determined by the approved findings of the board.

§ 940. Art. 140   Delegation by the President

The President may delegate any authority vested in him under this chapter, and provide for the subdelegation of any such authority.

SUBCHAPTER XII.   COURT OF APPEALS FOR THE ARMED FORCES

§ 941. Art. 141   Status

There is a court of record known as the United States Court of Appeals for the

Armed Forces. The court is established under article I of the Constitution. The court is located for administrative purposes only in the Department of Defense.

§ 942. Art. 142   Judges

(a) Number. The United States Court of Appeals for the Armed Forces consists of five judges.

(b) Appointment; qualification.

(1) Each judge of the court shall be appointed from civilian life by the President, by and with the advice and consent of the Senate, for a specified term determined under paragraph (2). A judge may serve as a senior judge as provided in subsection (e).

(2) The term of a judge shall expire as follows:

(A) In the case of a judge who is appointed after March 31 and before October 1 of any year, the term shall expire on September 30 of the year in which the fifteenth anniversary of the appointment occurs.

(B) In the case of a judge who is appointed after September 30 of any year and before April 1 of the following year, the term shall expire fifteen years after such September 30.

(3) Not more than three of the judges of the court may be appointed from the same political party, and no person may be appointed to be a judge of the court unless the person is a member of the bar of a Federal court or the highest court of a State.

(4) For purposes of appointment of judges to the court, a person retired from the armed forces after 20 or more years of active service (whether or not such person is on the retired list) shall not be considered to be in civilian life.

(c) Removal. Judges of the court may be removed from office by the President, upon notice and hearing, for —

(1) neglect of duty;

(2) misconduct; or

(3) mental or physical disability.

A judge may not be removed by the President for any other cause.

(d) Pay and allowances. Each judge of the court is entitled to the same salary and travel allowances as are, and from time to time may be, provided for judges of the United States Courts of Appeals.

(e) Senior judges.

(1) (A) A former judge of the court who is receiving retired pay or an annuity under section 945 of this title (article 145) or under subchapter III of chapter 83 or chapter 84 of title 5 shall be a senior judge. The chief judge of the court may call upon an individual who is a senior judge of the court under this subparagraph, with the consent of the senior judge, to perform judicial duties with the court —

(i) during a period a judge of the court is unable to perform his duties because of illness or other disability;

(ii) during a period in which a position of judge of the court is vacant; or

(iii) in any case in which a judge of the court recuses himself.

(B) If, at the time the term of a judge expires, no successor to that judge has been appointed, the chief judge of the court may call upon that judge (with that judge's consent) to continue to perform judicial duties with the court until the vacancy is filled. A judge who, upon the expiration of the judge's term, continues to perform judicial duties with the court without a break in service under this subparagraph shall be a senior judge while such service continues.

(2) A senior judge shall be paid for each day on which he performs judicial duties with the court an amount equal to the daily equivalent of the annual rate of pay provided for a judge of the court. Such pay shall be in lieu of retired pay and in lieu of an annuity under section 945 of this title (article 145), subchapter III of chapter 83 or subchapter II of chapter 84 of title 5, or any other retirement system for employees of the Federal Government.

(3) A senior judge, while performing duties referred to in paragraph (1), shall be provided with such office space and staff assistance as the chief judge considers appropriate and shall be entitled to the per diem, travel allowances, and other allowances provided for judges of the court.

(4) A senior judge shall be considered to be an officer or employee of the United States with respect to his status as a senior judge, but only during periods the senior judge is performing duties referred to in paragraph (1). For the purposes of section 205 of title 18, a senior judge shall be considered to be a special government employee during such periods. Any provision of law that prohibits or limits the political or business activities of an employee of the United States shall apply to a senior judge only during such periods.

(5) The court shall prescribe rules for the use and conduct of senior judges of the court. The chief judge of the court shall transmit such rules, and any amendments to such rules, to the Committee on Armed Services of the Senate and the Committee on Armed Services of the House of Representatives not later than 15 days after the issuance of such rules or amendments, as the case may be.

(6) For purposes of subchapter III of chapter 83 of title 5 (relating to the Civil Service Retirement and Disability System) and chapter 84 of such title (relating to the Federal Employees' Retirement System) and for purposes of any other Federal Government retirement system for employees of the Federal Government —

(A) a period during which a senior judge performs duties referred to in paragraph (1) shall not be considered creditable service;

(B) no amount shall be withheld from the pay of a senior judge as a retirement contribution under section 8334, 8343, 8422, or 8432 of title 5 or under any other such retirement system for any period during which the senior judge performs duties referred to in paragraph (1);

(C) no contribution shall be made by the Federal Government to any retirement system with respect to a senior judge for any period during which the senior judge performs duties referred to in paragraph (1); and

(D) a senior judge shall not be considered to be a reemployed annuitant for any period during which the senior judge performs duties referred to in paragraph (1).

(f) Service of Article III judges.

(1) The Chief Justice of the United States, upon the request of the chief judge of the court, may designate a judge of a United States court of appeals or of a United States district court to perform the duties of judge of the United States Court of Appeals for the Armed Forces —

(A) during a period a judge of the court is unable to perform his duties because of illness or other disability;

(B) in any case in which a judge of the court recuses himself; or

(C) during a period when there is a vacancy on the court and in the opinion of the chief judge of the court such a designation is necessary for the proper dispatch of the business of the court.

(2) The chief judge of the court may not request that a designation be made under paragraph (1) unless the chief judge has determined that no person is available to perform judicial duties with the court as a senior judge under subsection (e).

(3) A designation under paragraph (1) may be made only with the consent of the designated judge and the concurrence of the chief judge of the court of appeals or district court concerned.

(4) Per diem, travel allowances, and other allowances paid to the designated judge in connection with the performance of duties for the court shall be paid from funds available for the payment of per diem and such allowances for judges of the court.

(g) Effect of vacancy on court. A vacancy on the court does not impair the right of the remaining judges to exercise the powers of the court.

§ 943. Art. 143 Organization and employees

(a) Chief judge.

(1) The chief judge of the United States Court of Appeals for the Armed Forces shall be the judge of the court in regular active service who is senior in commission among the judges of the court who —

(A) have served for one or more years as judges of the court; and

(B) have not previously served as chief judge.

(2) In any case in which there is no judge of the court in regular active service who has served as a judge of the court for at least one year, the judge of the court in regular active service who is senior in commission and has not served previously as chief judge shall act as the chief judge.

(3) Except as provided in paragraph (4), a judge of the court shall serve as the chief judge under paragraph (1) for a term of five years. If no other judge is eligible under paragraph (1) to serve as chief judge upon the expiration of that term, the chief judge shall continue to serve as chief judge until another judge becomes eligible under that paragraph to serve as chief judge.

(4) (A) The term of a chief judge shall be terminated before the end of five years if —

(i) the chief judge leaves regular active service as a judge of the court; or

(ii) the chief judge notifies the other judges of the court in writing that such judge desires to be relieved of his duties as chief judge.

(B) The effective date of a termination of the term under subparagraph (A) shall be the date on which the chief judge leaves regular active service or the date of the notification under subparagraph (A)(ii), as the case may be.

(5) If a chief judge is temporarily unable to perform his duties as a chief judge, the duties shall be performed by the judge of the court in active service who is present, able and qualified to act, and is next in precedence.

(b) Precedence of judges. The chief judge of the court shall have precedence and preside at any session that he attends. The other judges shall have precedence and preside according to the seniority of their original commissions. Judges whose commissions bear the same date shall have precedence according to seniority in age.

(c) Status of certain positions.

(1) Attorney positions of employment under the Court of Appeals for the Armed Forces are excepted from the competitive service. A position of employment under the court that is provided primarily for the service of one judge of the court, reports directly to the judge, and is a position of a confidential character is excepted from the competitive service. Appointments to positions referred to in the preceding sentences shall be made by the court, without the concurrence of any other officer or employee of the executive branch, in the same manner as appointments are made to other executive branch positions of a confidential or policy-determining character for which it is not practicable to examine or to hold a competitive examination. Such positions shall not be counted as positions of that character for purposes of any limitation on the number of positions of that character provided in law.

(2) In making appointments to the positions described in paragraph (1), preference shall be given, among equally qualified persons, to persons who are preference eligibles (as defined in section 2108(3) of title 5).

§ 944. Art. 144   Procedure

The United States Court of Appeals for the Armed Forces may prescribe its rules of procedure and may determine the number of judges required to constitute a quorum.

§ 945. Art. 145   Annuities for judges and survivors

(a) Retirement annuities for judges.

(1) A person who has completed a term of service for which he was appointed as a judge of the United States Court of Appeals for the Armed Forces is eligible for an annuity under this section upon separation from civilian service in the Federal Government. A person who continues service with the court as a senior judge under section 942(e)(1)(B) of this title (article 142(e)(1)(B)) upon the expiration of the judge's term shall be considered to have been separated from civilian service in the Federal Government only upon the termination of that continuous service.

(2) A person who is eligible for an annuity under this section shall be paid that annuity if, at the time he becomes eligible to receive that annuity, he elects to receive that annuity in lieu of any other annuity for which he may be eligible at the time of such election (whether an immediate or a deferred annuity) under subchapter III of chapter 83 or subchapter II of chapter 84 of title 5 or any other retirement system for civilian employees of the Federal Government. Such an election may not be revoked.

(3) (A) The Secretary of Defense shall notify the Director of the Office of Personnel Management whenever an election under paragraph (2) is made affecting any right or interest under subchapter III of chapter 83 or subchapter II of chapter 84 of title 5 based on service as a judge of the United States Court of Appeals for the Armed Forces.

(B) Upon receiving any notification under subparagraph (A) in the case of a person making an election under paragraph (2), the Director shall determine the amount of the person's lump-sum credit under subchapter III of chapter 83 or subchapter II of chapter 84 of title 5, as applicable, and shall request the Secretary of the Treasury to transfer such amount from the Civil Service Retirement and Disability Fund to the Department of Defense Military Retirement Fund. The Secretary of the Treasury shall make any transfer so requested.

(C) In determining the amount of a lump-sum credit under section 8331(8) of title 5 for purposes of this paragraph —

(i) interest shall be computed using the rates under section 8334(e)(3) of such title; and

(ii) the completion of 5 years of civilian service (or longer) shall not be a basis for excluding interest.

(b) Amount of annuity. The annuity payable under this section to a person who makes an election under subsection (a)(2) is 80 percent of the rate of pay for a judge in active service on the United States Court of Appeals for the Armed

Forces as of the date on which the person is separated from civilian service.

(c) Relation to thrift savings plan. Nothing in this section affects any right of any person to participate in the thrift savings plan under section 8351 of title 5 or subchapter III of chapter 84 of such title.

(d) Survivor annuities. The Secretary of Defense shall prescribe by regulation a program to provide annuities for survivors and former spouses of persons receiving annuities under this section by reason of elections made by such persons under subsection (a)(2). That program shall, to the maximum extent practicable, provide benefits and establish terms and conditions that are similar to those provided under survivor and former spouse annuity programs under other retirement systems for civilian employees of the Federal Government. The program may include provisions for the reduction in the annuity paid the person as a condition for the survivor annuity. An election by a judge (including a senior judge) or former judge to receive an annuity under this section terminates any right or interest which any other individual may have to a survivor annuity under any other retirement system for civilian employees of the Federal Government based on the service of that judge or former judge as a civilian officer or employee of the Federal Government (except with respect to an election under subsection (g)(1)(B)).

(e) Cost-of-living increases. The Secretary of Defense shall periodically increase annuities and survivor annuities paid under this section in order to take account of changes in the cost of living. The Secretary shall prescribe by regulation procedures for increases in annuities under this section. Such system shall, to the maximum extent appropriate, provide cost-of-living adjustments that are similar to those that are provided under other retirement systems for civilian employees of the Federal Government.

(f) Dual compensation. A person who is receiving an annuity under this section by reason of service as a judge of the court and who is appointed to a position in the Federal Government shall, during the period of such person's service in such position, be entitled to receive only the annuity under this section or the pay for that position, whichever is higher.

(g) Election of judicial retirement benefits.

(1) A person who is receiving an annuity under this section by reason of service as a judge of the court and who later is appointed as a justice or judge of the United States to hold office during good behavior and who retires from that office, or from regular active service in that office, shall be paid either (A) the annuity under this section, or (B) the annuity or salary to which he is entitled by reason of his service as such a justice or judge of the United States, as determined by an election by that person at the time of his retirement from the office, or from regular active service in the office, of justice or judge of the United States. Such an election may not be revoked.

(2) An election by a person to be paid an annuity or salary pursuant to paragraph (1)(B) terminates (A) any election previously made by such person to provide a survivor annuity pursuant to subsection (d), and (B) any right of any other individual to receive a survivor annuity pursuant to subsection (d) on

the basis of the service of that person.

(h) Source of payment of annuities. Annuities and survivor annuities paid under this section shall be paid out of the Department of Defense Military Retirement Fund.

(i) Eligibility to elect between retirement systems.

(1) This subsection applies with respect to any person who —

(A) prior to being appointed as a judge of the United States Court of Appeals for the Armed Forces, performed civilian service of a type making such person subject to the Civil Service Retirement System; and

(B) would be eligible to make an election under section 301(a)(2) of the Federal Employees' Retirement System Act of 1986, by virtue of being appointed as such a judge, but for the fact that such person has not had a break in service of sufficient duration to be considered someone who is being reemployed by the Federal Government.

(2) Any person with respect to whom this subsection applies shall be eligible to make an election under section 301(a)(2) of the Federal Employees' Retirement System Act of 1986 to the same extent and in the same manner (including subject to the condition set forth in section 301(d) of such Act) as if such person's appointment constituted reemployment with the Federal Government.

§ 946. Art. 146   Code committee

(a) Annual survey. A committee shall meet at least annually and shall make an annual comprehensive survey of the operation of this chapter.

(b) Composition of committee. The committee shall consist of —

(1) the judges of the United States Court of Appeals for the Armed Forces;

(2) the Judge Advocates General of the Army, Navy, and Air Force, the Chief Counsel of the Coast Guard, and the Staff Judge Advocate to the Commandant of the Marine Corps; and

(3) two members of the public appointed by the Secretary of Defense.

(c) Reports.

(1) After each such survey, the committee shall submit a report —

(A) to the Committee on Armed Services of the Senate and the Committee on Armed Services of the House of Representatives; and

(B) to the Secretary of Defense, the Secretaries of the military departments, and the Secretary of Homeland Security.

(2) Each report under paragraph (1) shall include the following:

(A) Information on the number and status of pending cases.

(B) Any recommendation of the committee relating to —

(i) uniformity of policies as to sentences;

(ii) amendments to this chapter; and

(iii) any other matter the committee considers appropriate.

(d) Qualifications and terms of appointed members. Each member of the committee appointed by the Secretary of Defense under subsection (b)(3) shall be a recognized authority in military justice or criminal law. Each such member shall be appointed for a term of three years.

(e) Applicability of Federal Advisory Committee Act. The Federal Advisory Committee Act (5 U.S.C. App. I) shall not apply to the committee.

MILITARY COMMISSIONS ACT OF 2009
10 U.S. Code ch. 47A

SUBCHAPTER I.   GENERAL PROVISIONS

§ 948a.   Definitions

In this chapter:

(1) ALIEN. — The term "alien" means an individual who is not a citizen of the United States.

(2) CLASSIFIED INFORMATION. — The term "classified information" means the following:

(A) Any information or material that has been determined by the United States Government pursuant to statute, Executive order, or regulation to require protection against unauthorized disclosure for reasons of national security.

(B) Any restricted data, as that term is defined in section 11 y. of the Atomic Energy Act of 1954 (42 U.S.C. 2014(y)).

(3) COALITION PARTNER. — The term "coalition partner", with respect to hostilities engaged in by the United States, means any State or armed force directly engaged along with the United States in such hostilities or providing direct operational support to the United States in connection with such hostilities.

(4) GENEVA CONVENTION RELATIVE TO THE TREATMENT OF PRISONERS OF WAR. — The term "Geneva Convention Relative to the Treatment of Prisoners of War" means the Convention Relative to the Treatment of Prisoners of War, done at Geneva August 12, 1949 (6 UST 3316).

(5) GENEVA CONVENTIONS. — The term "Geneva Conventions" means the international conventions signed at Geneva on August 12, 1949.

(6) PRIVILEGED BELLIGERENT. — The term "privileged belligerent" means an individual belonging to one of the eight categories enumerated in Article 4 of the Geneva Convention Relative to the Treatment of Prisoners of War.

(7) UNPRIVILEGED ENEMY BELLIGERENT. — The term "unprivileged enemy belligerent" means an individual (other than a privileged belligerent) who —

(A) has engaged in hostilities against the United States or its coalition partners;

(B) has purposefully and materially supported hostilities against the United States or its coalition partners; or

(C) was a part of al Qaeda at the time of the alleged offense under this chapter.

(8) NATIONAL SECURITY. — The term "national security" means the national defense and foreign relations of the United States.

(9) HOSTILITIES. — The term "hostilities" means any conflict subject to

the laws of war.

§ 948b. Military commissions generally

(a) PURPOSE. — This chapter establishes procedures governing the use of military commissions to try alien unprivileged enemy belligerents for violations of the law of war and other offenses triable by military commission.

(b) AUTHORITY FOR MILITARY COMMISSIONS UNDER THISCHAP-TER. — The President is authorized to establish military commissions under this chapter for offenses triable by military commission as provided in this chapter.

(c) CONSTRUCTION OF PROVISIONS. — The procedures for military commissions set forth in this chapter are based upon the procedures for trial by general courts-martial under chapter 47 of this title (the Uniform Code of Military Justice). Chapter 47 of this title does not, by its terms, apply to trial by military commission except as specifically provided therein or in this chapter, and many of the provisions of chapter 47 of this title are by their terms inapplicable to military commissions. The judicial construction and application of chapter 47 of this title, while instructive, is therefore not of its own force binding on military commissions established under this chapter.

(d) INAPPLICABILITY OF CERTAIN PROVISIONS. —

(1) The following provisions of this title shall not apply to trial by military commission under this chapter:

(A) Section 810 (article 10 of the Uniform Code of Military Justice), relating to speedy trial, including any rule of courts-martial relating to speedy trial.

(B) Sections 831(a), (b), and (d)(articles 31(a), (b), and (d) of the Uniform Code of Military Justice), relating to compulsory self-incrimination.

(C) Section 832 (article 32 of the Uniform Code of Military Justice), relating to pretrial investigation.

(2) Other provisions of chapter 47 of this title shall apply to trial by military commission under this chapter only to the extent provided by the terms of such provisions or by this chapter.

(e) GENEVA CONVENTIONS NOT ESTABLISHING PRIVATE RIGHT OF ACTION. — No alien unprivileged enemy belligerent subject to trial by military commission under this chapter may invoke the Geneva Conventions as a basis for a private right of action.

§ 948c. Persons subject to military commissions

Any alien unprivileged enemy belligerent is subject to trial by military commission as set forth in this chapter.

§ 948d. Jurisdiction of military commissions

A military commission under this chapter shall have jurisdiction to try persons subject to this chapter for any offense made punishable by this chapter, sections

904 and 906 of this title (articles 104 and 106 of the Uniform Code of Military Justice), or the law of war, whether such offense was committed before, on, or after September 11, 2001, and may, under such limitations as the President may prescribe, adjudge any punishment not forbidden by this chapter, including the penalty of death when specifically authorized under this chapter. A military commission is a competent tribunal to make a finding sufficient for jurisdiction.

SUBCHAPTER II. COMPOSITION OF MILITARY COMMISSIONS

§ 948h. Who may convene military commissions

Military commissions under this chapter may be convened by the Secretary of Defense or by any officer or official of the United States designated by the Secretary for that purpose.

§ 948i. Who may serve on military commissions

(a) IN GENERAL. — Any commissioned officer of the armed forces on active duty is eligible to serve on a military commission under this chapter, including commissioned officers of the reserve components

of the armed forces on active duty, commissioned officers of the National Guard on active duty in Federal service, or retired commissioned officers recalled to active duty.

(b) DETAIL OF MEMBERS. — When convening a military commission under this chapter, the convening authority shall detail as members thereof such members of the armed forces eligible under subsection (a) who, in the opinion of the convening authority, are best qualified for the duty by reason of age, education, training, experience, length of service, and judicial temperament. No member of an armed force is eligible to serve as a member of a military commission when such member is the accuser or a witness for the prosecution or has acted as an investigator or counsel in the same case.

(c) EXCUSE OF MEMBERS. — Before a military commission under this chapter is assembled for the trial of a case, the convening authority may excuse a member from participating in the case.

§ 948j. Military judge of a military commission

(a) DETAIL OF MILITARY JUDGE. — A military judge shall be detailed to each military commission under this chapter. The Secretary of Defense shall prescribe regulations providing for the manner in which military judges are so detailed to military commissions. The military judge shall preside over each military commission to which such military judge has been detailed.

(b) ELIGIBILITY. — A military judge shall be a commissioned officer of the armed forces who is a member of the bar of a Federal court, or a member of the bar of the highest court of a State, and who is certified to be qualified for duty under section 826 of this title (article 26 of the Uniform Code of Military Justice) as a military judge of general courts-martial by the Judge Advocate General of the armed force of which such military judge is a member.

(c) INELIGIBILITY OF CERTAIN INDIVIDUALS. — No person is eligible to act as military judge in a case of a military commission under this chapter if such person is the accuser or a witness or has acted as investigator or a counsel in the same case.

(d) CONSULTATION WITH MEMBERS; INELIGIBILITY TO VOTE. —

A military judge detailed to a military commission under this chapter may not consult with the members except in the presence of the accused (except as otherwise provided in section 949d of this title), trial counsel, and defense counsel, nor may such military judge vote with the members.

(e) OTHER DUTIES. — A commissioned officer who is certified to be qualified for duty as a military judge of a military commission under this chapter may perform such other duties as are assigned to such officer by or with the approval of the Judge Advocate General of the armed force of which such officer is a member or the designee of such Judge Advocate General.

(f) PROHIBITION ON EVALUATION OF FITNESS BY CONVENING AUTHORITY. — The convening authority of a military commission under this chapter may not prepare or review any report concerning the effectiveness, fitness, or efficiency of a military judge detailed to the military commission which relates to such judge's performance of duty as a military judge on the military commission.

§ 948k. Detail of trial counsel and defense counsel

(a) DETAIL OF COUNSEL GENERALLY. —

(1) Trial counsel and military defense counsel shall be detailed for each military commission under this chapter.

(2) Assistant trial counsel and assistant and associate defense counsel may be detailed for a military commission under this chapter.

(3) Military defense counsel for a military commission under this chapter shall be detailed as soon as practicable.

(4) The Secretary of Defense shall prescribe regulations providing for the manner in which trial counsel and military defense counsel are detailed for military commissions under this chapter and for the persons who are authorized to detail such counsel for such military commissions.

(b) TRIAL COUNSEL. — Subject to subsection (e), a trial counsel detailed for a military commission under this chapter shall be —

(1) a judge advocate (as that term is defined in section 801 of this title (article 1 of the Uniform Code of Military Justice)) who is —

(A) a graduate of an accredited law school or a member of the bar of a Federal court or of the highest court of a State; and

(B) certified as competent to perform duties as trial counsel before general courts-martial by the Judge Advocate General of the armed force of which such judge advocate is a member; or

(2) a civilian who is —

(A) a member of the bar of a Federal court or of the highest court of a State; and

(B) otherwise qualified to practice before the military commission pursuant to regulations prescribed by the Secretary of Defense.

(c) DEFENSE COUNSEL. —

(1) Subject to subsection (e), a military defense counsel detailed for a military commission under this chapter shall be a judge advocate (as so defined) who is —

(A) a graduate of an accredited law school or a member of the bar of a Federal court or of the highest court of a State; and

(B) certified as competent to perform duties as defense counsel before general courts-martial by the Judge Advocate General of the armed force of which such judge advocate is a member.

(2) The Secretary of Defense shall prescribe regulations for the appointment and performance of defense counsel in capital cases under this chapter.

(d) CHIEF PROSECUTOR; CHIEF DEFENSE COUNSEL. —

(1) The Chief Prosecutor in a military commission under this chapter shall meet the requirements set forth in subsection (b)(1).

(2) The Chief Defense Counsel in a military commission under this chapter shall meet the requirements set forth in subsection (c)(1).

(e) INELIGIBILITY OF CERTAIN INDIVIDUALS. — No person who has acted as an investigator, military judge, or member of a military commission under this chapter in any case may act later as trial counsel or military defense counsel in the same case. No person who has acted for the prosecution before a military commission under this chapter may act later in the same case for the defense, nor may any person who has acted for the defense before a military commission under this chapter act later in the same case for the prosecution.

§ 948l. Detail or employment of reporters and interpreters

(a) COURT REPORTERS. — Under such regulations as the Secretary of Defense may prescribe, the convening authority of a military commission under this chapter shall detail to or employ for the military commission qualified court reporters, who shall prepare a verbatim record of the proceedings of and testimony taken before the military commission.

(b) INTERPRETERS. — Under such regulations as the Secretary of Defense may prescribe, the convening authority of a military commission under this chapter may detail to or employ for the military commission interpreters who shall interpret for the military commission, and, as necessary, for trial counsel and defense counsel for the military commission, and for the accused.

(c) TRANSCRIPT; RECORD. — The transcript of a military commission under this chapter shall be under the control of the convening authority of the military commission, who shall also be responsible for preparing the record of the proceedings of the military commission.

§ 948m. Number of members; excuse of members; absent and additional members

(a) NUMBER OF MEMBERS. —

(1) Except as provided in paragraph (2), a military commission under this chapter shall have at least five members.

(2) In a case in which the accused before a military commission under this chapter may be sentenced to a penalty of death, the military commission shall have the number of members prescribed by section 949m(c) of this title.

(b) EXCUSE OF MEMBERS. — No member of a military commission under this chapter may be absent or excused after the military commission has been assembled for the trial of a case unless excused —

(1) as a result of challenge;

(2) by the military judge for physical disability or other good cause; or

(3) by order of the convening authority for good cause.

(c) ABSENT AND ADDITIONAL MEMBERS. — Whenever a military commission under this chapter is reduced below the number of members required by subsection (a), the trial may not proceed unless the convening authority details new members sufficient to provide not less than such number. The trial may proceed with the new members present after the recorded evidence previously introduced before the members has been read to the military commission in the presence of the military judge, the accused (except as provided in section 949d of this title), and counsel for both sides.

SUBCHAPTER III. PRE-TRIAL PROCEDURE

§ 948q. Charges and specifications

(a) CHARGES AND SPECIFICATIONS. — Charges and specifications against an accused in a military commission under this chapter shall be signed by a person subject to chapter 47 of this title under oath before a commissioned officer of the armed forces authorized to administer oaths and shall state —

(1) that the signer has personal knowledge of, or reason to believe, the matters set forth therein; and

(2) that such matters are true in fact to the best of the signer's knowledge and belief.

(b) NOTICE TO ACCUSED. — Upon the swearing of the charges and specifications in accordance with subsection (a), the accused shall be informed of the charges and specifications against the accused as soon as practicable.

§ 948r. Exclusion of statements obtained by torture or cruel, inhuman, or degrading treatment; prohibition of self-incrimination; admission of other statements of the accused

(a) EXCLUSION OF STATEMENTS OBTAINED BY TORTURE OR CRUEL, INHUMAN, OR DEGRADING TREATMENT. — No statement obtained by the use of torture or by cruel, inhuman, or degrading treatment (as defined by section 1003 of the Detainee Treatment Act of 2005 (42 U.S.C. 2000dd)), whether or not under color of law, shall be admissible in a military commission under this chapter, except against a person accused of torture or such treatment as evidence that the statement was made.

(b) SELF-INCRIMINATION PROHIBITED. — No person shall be required to testify against himself or herself at a proceeding of a military commission under this chapter.

(c) OTHER STATEMENTS OF THE ACCUSED. — A statement of the accused may be admitted in evidence in a military commission under this chapter only if the military judge finds —

(1) that the totality of the circumstances renders the statement reliable and possessing sufficient probative value; and

(2) that —

(A) the statement was made incident to lawful conduct during military operations at the point of capture or during closely related active combat engagement, and the interests of justice would best be served by admission of the statement into evidence; or

(B) the statement was voluntarily given.

(d) DETERMINATION OF VOLUNTARINESS. — In determining for purposes of subsection (c)(2)(B) whether a statement was voluntarily given, the military judge shall consider the totality of the circumstances, including, as appropriate, the following:

(1) The details of the taking of the statement, accounting for the circumstances of the conduct of military and intelligence operations during hostilities.

(2) The characteristics of the accused, such as military training, age, and education level.

(3) The lapse of time, change of place, or change in identity of the questioners between the statement sought to be admitted and any prior questioning of the accused.

§ 948s. Service of charges

The trial counsel assigned to a case before a military commission under this chapter shall cause to be served upon the accused and military defense counsel a copy of the charges upon which trial is to be had in English and, if appropriate, in another language that the accused understands, sufficiently in advance of trial to prepare a defense.

SUBCHAPTER IV. TRIAL PROCEDURE

§ 949a. Rules

(a) PROCEDURES AND RULES OF EVIDENCE. — Pretrial, trial, and post-trial procedures, including elements and modes of proof, for cases triable by military commission under this chapter may be prescribed by the Secretary of Defense. Such procedures may not be contrary to or inconsistent with this chapter. Except as otherwise provided in this chapter or chapter 47 of this title, the procedures and rules of evidence applicable in trials by general courts-martial of the United States shall apply in trials by military commission under this chapter.

(b) EXCEPTIONS. —

(1) In trials by military commission under this chapter, the Secretary of Defense, in consultation with the Attorney General, may make such exceptions in the applicability of the procedures and rules of evidence otherwise applicable in general courts-martial as may be required by the unique circumstances of the conduct of military and intelligence operations during hostilities or by other practical need consistent with this chapter.

(2) Notwithstanding any exceptions authorized by paragraph (1), the procedures and rules of evidence in trials by military commission under this chapter shall include, at a minimum, the following rights of the accused:

(A) To present evidence in the accused's defense, to cross-examine the witnesses who testify against the accused, and to examine and respond to all evidence admitted against the accused on the issue of guilt or innocence and for sentencing, as provided for by this chapter.

(B) To be present at all sessions of the military commission (other than those for deliberations or voting), except when excluded under section 949d of this title.

(C) (i) When none of the charges preferred against the accused are capital, to be represented before a military commission by civilian counsel if provided at no expense to the Government, and by either the defense counsel detailed or the military counsel of the accused's own selection, if reasonably available.

(ii) When any of the charges preferred against the accused are capital, to be represented before a military commission in accordance with clause (i) and, to the greatest extent practicable, by at least one additional counsel who is learned in applicable law relating to capital cases and who, if necessary, may be a civilian and compensated in accordance with regulations prescribed by the Secretary of Defense.

(D) To self-representation, if the accused knowingly and competently waives the assistance of counsel, subject to the provisions of paragraph (4).

(E) To the suppression of evidence that is not reliable or probative.

(F) To the suppression of evidence the probative value of which is substantially outweighed by —

(i) the danger of unfair prejudice, confusion of the issues, or misleading the members; or

(ii) considerations of undue delay, waste of time, or needless presentation of cumulative evidence.

(3) In making exceptions in the applicability in trials by military commission under this chapter from the procedures and rules otherwise applicable in general courts-martial, the Secretary of Defense may provide the following:

(A) Evidence seized outside the United States shall not be excluded from trial by military commission on the grounds that the evidence was not seized pursuant to a search warrant or authorization.

(B) A statement of the accused that is otherwise admissible shall not be excluded from trial by military commission on grounds of alleged coercion or compulsory self-incrimination so long as the evidence complies with the provisions of section 948r of this title.

(C) Evidence shall be admitted as authentic so long as —

(i) the military judge of the military commission determines that there is sufficient evidence that the evidence is what it is claimed to be; and

(ii) the military judge instructs the members that they may consider any issue as to authentication or identification of evidence in determining the weight, if any, to be given to the evidence.

(D) Hearsay evidence not otherwise admissible under the rules of evidence applicable in trial by general courts-martial may be admitted in a trial by military commission only if —

(i) the proponent of the evidence makes known to the adverse party, sufficiently in advance to provide the adverse party with a fair opportunity to meet the evidence, the proponent's intention to offer the evidence, and the particulars of the evidence (including information on the circumstances under which the evidence was obtained); and

(ii) the military judge, after taking into account all of the circumstances surrounding the taking of the statement, including the degree to which the statement is corroborated, the indicia of reliability within the statement itself, and whether the will of the declarant was overborne, determines that —

(I) the statement is offered as evidence of a material fact;

(II) the statement is probative on the point for which it is offered;

(III) direct testimony from the witness is not available as a practical matter, taking into consideration the physical location of the witness, the unique circumstances of military and intelligence operations during hostilities, and the adverse impacts on military or intelligence operations that would likely result from the production of the witness;

and

(IV) the general purposes of the rules of evidence and the interests of justice will best be served by admission of the statement into evidence.

(4) (A) The accused in a military commission under this chapter who exercises the right to self-representation under paragraph (2)(D) shall conform the accused's deportment and the conduct of the defense to the rules of evidence, procedure, and decorum applicable to trials by military commission.

(B) Failure of the accused to conform to the rules described in subparagraph (A) may result in a partial or total revocation by the military judge of the right of self-representation under paragraph (2)(D). In such case, the military counsel of the accused or an appropriately authorized civilian counsel shall perform the functions necessary for the defense.

(c) DELEGATION OF AUTHORITY TO PRESCRIBE REGULATIONS. — The Secretary of Defense may delegate the authority of the Secretary to prescribe regulations under this chapter.

(d) NOTICE TO CONGRESS OF MODIFICATION OF RULES. — Not later than 60 days before the date on which any proposed modification of the rules in effect for military commissions under this chapter goes into effect, the Secretary of Defense shall submit to the Committee on Armed Services of the Senate and the Committee on Armed Services of the House of Representatives a report describing the proposed modification.

§ 949b. Unlawfully influencing action of military commission and United States Court of Military Commission Review

(a) MILITARY COMMISSIONS. —

(1) No authority convening a military commission under this chapter may censure, reprimand, or admonish the military commission, or any member, military judge, or counsel thereof, with respect to the findings or sentence adjudged by the military commission, or with respect to any other exercises of its or their functions in the conduct of the proceedings.

(2) No person may attempt to coerce or, by any unauthorized means, influence —

(A) the action of a military commission under this chapter, or any member thereof, in reaching the findings or sentence in any case;

(B) the action of any convening, approving, or reviewing authority with respect to their judicial acts; or

(C) the exercise of professional judgment by trial counsel or defense counsel.

(3) The provisions of this subsection shall not apply with respect to —

(A) general instructional or informational courses in military justice if such courses are designed solely for the purpose of instructing members of a command in the substantive and procedural aspects of military commissions; or

(B) statements and instructions given in open proceedings by a military judge or counsel.

(b) UNITED STATES COURT OF MILITARY COMMISSION REVIEW.

(1) No person may attempt to coerce or, by any unauthorized means, influence —

(A) the action of a military appellate judge or other duly appointed judge under this chapter on the United States Court of Military Commissions Review in reaching a decision on the findings or sentence on appeal in any case; or

(B) the exercise of professional judgment by trial counsel or defense counsel appearing before the United States Court of Military Commission Review.

(2) No person may censure, reprimand, or admonish a military appellate judge on the United States Court of Military Commission Review, or counsel thereof, with respect to any exercise of their functions in the conduct of proceedings under this chapter.

(3) The provisions of this subsection shall not apply with respect to —

(A) general instructional or informational courses in military justice if such courses are designed solely for the purpose of instructing members of a command in the substantive and procedural aspects of military commissions; or

(B) statements and instructions given in open proceedings by an appellate military judge or a duly appointed appellate judge on the United States Court of Military Commission Review, or counsel.

(4) No appellate military judge on the United States Court of Military Commission Review may be reassigned to other duties, except under circumstances as follows:

(A) The appellate military judge voluntarily requests to be reassigned to other duties and the Secretary of Defense, or the designee of the Secretary, in consultation with the Judge Advocate General of the armed force of which the appellate military judge is a member, approves such reassignment.

(B) The appellate military judge retires or otherwise separates from the armed forces.

(C) The appellate military judge is reassigned to other duties by the Secretary of Defense, or the designee of the Secretary, in consultation with the Judge Advocate General of the armed force of which the appellate military judge is a member, based on military necessity and such reassignment is consistent with service rotation regulations (to the extent such regulations are applicable).

(D) The appellate military judge is withdrawn by the Secretary of Defense, or the designee of the Secretary, in consultation with the Judge Advocate General of the armed force of which the appellate military judge is a member, for good cause consistent with applicable procedures under chapter 47 of this title (the Uniform Code of Military Justice).

(c) PROHIBITION ON CONSIDERATION OF ACTIONS ON COMMIS-SION IN EVALUATION OF FITNESS. — In the preparation of an effectiveness, fitness, or efficiency report or any other report or document used in whole or in part for the purpose of determining whether a commissioned officer of the armed forces is qualified to be advanced in grade, or in determining the assignment or transfer of any such officer or whether any such officer should be retained on active duty, no person may —

(1) consider or evaluate the performance of duty of any member of a military commission under this chapter; or

(2) give a less favorable rating or evaluation to any commissioned officer because of the zeal with which such officer, in acting as counsel, represented any accused before a military commission under this chapter.

§ 949c.   Duties of trial counsel and defense counsel

(a) TRIAL COUNSEL. — The trial counsel of a military commission under this chapter shall prosecute in the name of the United States.

(b) DEFENSE COUNSEL. —

(1) The accused shall be represented in the accused's defense before a military commission under this chapter as provided in this subsection.

(2) The accused may be represented by military counsel detailed under section 948k of this title or by military counsel of the accused's own selection, if reasonably available.

(3) The accused may be represented by civilian counsel if retained by the accused, provided that such civilian counsel —

(A) is a United States citizen;

(B) is admitted to the practice of law in a State, district, or possession of the United States, or before a Federal court;

(C) has not been the subject of any sanction of disciplinary action by any court, bar, or other competent governmental authority for relevant misconduct;

(D) has been determined to be eligible for access to information classified at the level Secret or higher; and

(E) has signed a written agreement to comply with all applicable regulations or instructions for counsel, including any rules of court for conduct during the proceedings.

(4) If the accused is represented by civilian counsel, military counsel shall act as associate counsel.

(5) The accused is not entitled to be represented by more than one military counsel. However, the person authorized under regulations prescribed under section 948k of this title to detail counsel, in such person's sole discretion, may detail additional military counsel to represent the accused.

(6) Defense counsel may cross-examine each witness for the prosecution who testifies before a military commission under this chapter.

(7) Civilian defense counsel shall protect any classified information received during the course of representation of the accused in accordance with all applicable law governing the protection of classified information, and may not divulge such information to any person not authorized to receive it.

§ 949d.   Sessions

(a) SESSIONS WITHOUT PRESENCE OF MEMBERS. —

(1) At any time after the service of charges which have been referred for trial by military commission under this chapter, the military judge may call the military commission into session without the presence of the members for the purpose of —

(A) hearing and determining motions raising defenses or objections which are capable of determination without trial of the issues raised by a plea of not guilty;

(B) hearing and ruling upon any matter which may be ruled upon by the military judge under this chapter, whether or not the matter is appropriate for later consideration or decision by the members;

(C) if permitted by regulations prescribed by the Secretary of Defense, receiving the pleas of the accused; and

(D) performing any other procedural function which may be performed by the military judge under this chapter or under rules prescribed pursuant to section 949a of this title and which does not require the presence of the members.

(2) Except as provided in subsections (b), (c), and (d), any proceedings under paragraph (1) shall be conducted in the presence of the accused, defense counsel, and trial counsel, and shall be made part of the record.

(b) DELIBERATION OR VOTE OF MEMBERS. — When the members of a military commission under this chapter deliberate or vote, only the members may be present.

(c) CLOSURE OF PROCEEDINGS. —

(1) The military judge may close to the public all or part of the proceedings of a military commission under this chapter.

(2) The military judge may close to the public all or a portion of the proceedings under paragraph (1) only upon making a specific finding that such closure is necessary to —

(A) protect information the disclosure of which could reasonably be expected to cause damage to the national security, including intelligence or law enforcement sources, methods, or activities; or

(B) ensure the physical safety of individuals.

(3) A finding under paragraph (2) may be based upon a presentation, including a presentation ex parte or in camera, by either trial counsel or defense counsel.

(d) EXCLUSION OF ACCUSED FROM CERTAIN PROCEEDINGS. — The military judge may exclude the accused from any portion of a proceeding upon a determination that, after being warned by the military judge, the accused persists in conduct that justifies exclusion from the courtroom —

(1) to ensure the physical safety of individuals; or

(2) to prevent disruption of the proceedings by the accused.

§ 949e. Continuances

The military judge in a military commission under this chapter may, for reasonable cause, grant a continuance to any party for such time, and as often, as may appear to be just.

§ 949f. Challenges

(a) CHALLENGES AUTHORIZED. — The military judge and members of a military commission under this chapter may be challenged by the accused or trial counsel for cause stated to the military commission. The military judge shall determine the relevance and validity of challenges for cause, and may not receive a challenge to more than one person at a time. Challenges by trial counsel shall ordinarily be presented and decided before those by the accused are offered.

(b) PEREMPTORY CHALLENGES. — The accused and trial counsel are each entitled to one peremptory challenge, but the military judge may not be challenged except for cause.

(c) CHALLENGES AGAINST ADDITIONAL MEMBERS. — Whenever additional members are detailed to a military commission under this chapter, and after any challenges for cause against such additional members are presented and decided, the accused and trial counsel are each entitled to one peremptory challenge against members not previously subject to peremptory challenge.

§ 949g. Oaths

(a) IN GENERAL. —

(1) Before performing their respective duties in a military commission under this chapter, military judges, members, trial counsel, defense counsel, reporters, and interpreters shall take an oath to perform their duties faithfully.

(2) The form of the oath required by paragraph (1), the time and place of the taking thereof, the manner of recording thereof, and whether the oath shall be taken for all cases in which duties are to be performed or for a particular case, shall be as provided in regulations prescribed by the Secretary of Defense. The

regulations may provide that —

(A) an oath to perform faithfully duties as a military judge, trial counsel, or defense counsel may be taken at any time by any judge advocate or other person certified to be qualified or competent for the duty; and

(B) if such an oath is taken, such oath need not again be taken at the time the judge advocate or other person is detailed to that duty.

(b) WITNESSES. — Each witness before a military commission under this chapter shall be examined on oath.

(c) OATH DEFINED. — In this section, the term "oath" includes an affirmation.

§ 949h.   Former jeopardy

(a) IN GENERAL. — No person may, without the person's consent, be tried by a military commission under this chapter a second time for the same offense.

(b) SCOPE OF TRIAL. — No proceeding in which the accused has been found guilty by military commission under this chapter upon any charge or specification is a trial in the sense of this section until the finding of guilty has become final after review of the case has been fully completed.

§ 949i.   Pleas of the accused

(a) PLEA OF NOT GUILTY. — If an accused in a military commission under this chapter after a plea of guilty sets up matter inconsistent with the plea, or if it appears that the accused has entered the plea of guilty through lack of understanding of its meaning and effect, or if the accused fails or refuses to plead, a plea of not guilty shall be entered in the record, and the military commission shall proceed as though the accused had pleaded not guilty.

(b) FINDING OF GUILT AFTER GUILTY PLEA. — With respect to any charge or specification to which a plea of guilty has been made by the accused in a military commission under this chapter and accepted by the military judge, a finding of guilty of the charge or specification may be entered immediately without a vote.

The finding shall constitute the finding of the military commission unless the plea of guilty is withdrawn prior to announcement of the sentence, in which event the proceedings shall continue as though the accused had pleaded not guilty.

§ 949j.   Opportunity to obtain witnesses and other evidence

(a) IN GENERAL. —

(1) Defense counsel in a military commission under this chapter shall have a reasonable opportunity to obtain witnesses and other evidence as provided in regulations prescribed by the Secretary of Defense. The opportunity to obtain witnesses and evidence shall be comparable to the opportunity available to a criminal defendant in a court of the United States under article III of the Constitution.

(2) Process issued in military commissions under this chapter to compel witnesses to appear and testify and to compel the production of other evidence —

(A) shall be similar to that which courts of the United States having criminal jurisdiction may lawfully issue; and

(B) shall run to any place where the United States shall have jurisdiction thereof.

(b) DISCLOSURE OF EXCULPATORY EVIDENCE. —

(1) As soon as practicable, trial counsel in a military commission under this chapter shall disclose to the defense the existence of any evidence that reasonably tends to —

(A) negate the guilt of the accused of an offense charged; or

(B) reduce the degree of guilt of the accused with respect to an offense charged.

(2) The trial counsel shall, as soon as practicable, disclose to the defense the existence of evidence that reasonably tends to impeach the credibility of a witness whom the government intends to call at trial.

(3) The trial counsel shall, as soon as practicable upon a finding of guilt, disclose to the defense the existence of evidence that is not subject to paragraph (1) or paragraph (2) but that reasonably may be viewed as mitigation evidence at sentencing.

(4) The disclosure obligations under this subsection encompass evidence that is known or reasonably should be known to any government officials who participated in the investigation and prosecution of the case against the defendant.

§ 949k. Defense of lack of mental responsibility

(a) AFFIRMATIVE DEFENSE. — It is an affirmative defense in a trial by military commission under this chapter that, at the time of the commission of the acts constituting the offense, the accused, as a result of a severe mental disease or defect, was unable to appreciate the nature and quality or the wrongfulness of the acts. Mental disease or defect does not otherwise constitute a defense.

(b) BURDEN OF PROOF. — The accused in a military commission under this chapter has the burden of proving the defense of lack of mental responsibility by clear and convincing evidence.

(c) FINDINGS FOLLOWING ASSERTION OF DEFENSE. — Whenever lack of mental responsibility of the accused with respect to an offense is properly at issue in a military commission under this chapter, the military judge shall instruct the members as to the defense of lack of mental responsibility under this section and shall charge the members to find the accused —

(1) guilty;

(2) not guilty; or

(3) subject to subsection (d), not guilty by reason of lack of mental responsibility.

(d) MAJORITY VOTE REQUIRED FOR FINDING. — The accused shall be found not guilty by reason of lack of mental responsibility under subsection (c)(3) only if a majority of the members present at the time the vote is taken determines that the defense of lack of mental responsibility has been established.

§ 949l. Voting and rulings

(a) VOTE BY SECRET WRITTEN BALLOT. — Voting by members of a military commission under this chapter on the findings and on the sentence shall be by secret written ballot.

(b) RULINGS. —

(1) The military judge in a military commission under this chapter shall rule upon all questions of law, including the admissibility of evidence and all interlocutory questions arising during the proceedings.

(2) Any ruling made by the military judge upon a question of law or an interlocutory question (other than the factual issue of mental responsibility of the accused) is conclusive and constitutes the ruling of the military commission. However, a military judge may change such a ruling at any time during the trial.

(c) INSTRUCTIONS PRIOR TO VOTE. — Before a vote is taken of the findings of a military commission under this chapter, the military judge shall, in the presence of the accused and counsel, instruct the members as to the elements of the offense and charge the members —

(1) that the accused must be presumed to be innocent until the accused's guilt is established by legal and competent evidence beyond a reasonable doubt;

(2) that in the case being considered, if there is a reasonable doubt as to the guilt of the accused, the doubt must be resolved in favor of the accused and the accused must be acquitted;

(3) that, if there is reasonable doubt as to the degree of guilt, the finding must be in a lower degree as to which there is no reasonable doubt; and

(4) that the burden of proof to establish the guilt of the accused beyond a reasonable doubt is upon the United States.

§ 949m. Number of votes required

(a) CONVICTION. — No person may be convicted by a military commission under this chapter of any offense, except as provided in section 949i(b) of this title or by concurrence of two-thirds of the members present at the time the vote is taken.

(b) SENTENCES. —

(1) Except as provided in paragraphs (2) and (3), sentences shall be

determined by a military commission by the concurrence of two-thirds of the members present at the time the vote is taken.

(2) No person may be sentenced to death by a military commission, except insofar as —

(A) the penalty of death has been expressly authorized under this chapter, chapter 47 of this title, or the law of war for an offense of which the accused has been found guilty;

(B) trial counsel expressly sought the penalty of death by filing an appropriate notice in advance of trial;

(C) the accused was convicted of the offense by the concurrence of all the members present at the time the vote is taken; and

(D) all members present at the time the vote was taken concurred in the sentence of death.

(3) No person may be sentenced to life imprisonment, or to confinement for more than 10 years, by a military commission under this chapter except by the concurrence of three-fourths of the members present at the time the vote is taken.

(c) NUMBER OF MEMBERS REQUIRED FOR PENALTY OF DEATH. —

(1) Except as provided in paragraph (2), in a case in which the penalty of death is sought, the number of members of the military commission under this chapter shall be not less than 12 members.

(2) In any case described in paragraph (1) in which 12 members are not reasonably available for a military commission because of physical conditions or military exigencies, the convening authority shall specify a lesser number of members for the military commission (but not fewer than 9 members), and the military commission may be assembled, and the trial held, with not less than the number of members so specified. In any such case, the convening authority shall make a detailed written statement, to be appended to the record, stating why a greater number of members were not reasonably available.

§ 949n. Military commission to announce action

A military commission under this chapter shall announce its findings and sentence to the parties as soon as determined.

§ 949o. Record of trial

(a) RECORD; AUTHENTICATION. — Each military commission under this chapter shall keep a separate, verbatim, record of the proceedings in each case brought before it, and the record shall be authenticated by the signature of the military judge. If the record cannot be authenticated by the military judge by reason of death, disability, or absence, it shall be authenticated by the signature of the trial counsel or by a member of the commission if the trial counsel is unable to authenticate it by reason of death, disability, or absence. Where appropriate, and as provided in regulations prescribed by the Secretary of Defense, the record of a military commission under this chapter may contain a classified annex.

(b) COMPLETE RECORD REQUIRED. — A complete record of the proceedings and testimony shall be prepared in every military commission under this chapter.

(c) PROVISION OF COPY TO ACCUSED. — A copy of the record of the proceedings of the military commission under this chapter shall be given the accused as soon as it is authenticated. If the record contains classified information, or a classified annex, the accused shall receive a redacted version of the record consistent with the requirements of subchapter V of this chapter. Defense counsel shall have access to the unredacted record, as provided in regulations prescribed by the Secretary of Defense.

SUBCHAPTER V.   CLASSIFIED INFORMATION PROCEDURES

§ 949p–1.   Protection of classified information: applicability of subchapter

(a) PROTECTION OF CLASSIFIED INFORMATION. — Classified information shall be protected and is privileged from disclosure if disclosure would be detrimental to the national security. Under no circumstances may a military judge order the release of classified information to any person not authorized to receive such information.

(b) ACCESS TO EVIDENCE. — Any information admitted into evidence pursuant to any rule, procedure, or order by the military judge shall be provided to the accused.

(c) DECLASSIFICATION. — Trial counsel shall work with the original classification authorities for evidence that may be used at trial to ensure that such evidence is declassified to the maximum extent possible, consistent with the requirements of national security. A decision not to declassify evidence under this section shall not be subject to review by a military commission or upon appeal.

(d) CONSTRUCTION OF PROVISIONS. — The judicial construction of the Classified Information Procedures Act (18 U.S.C. App.) shall be authoritative in the interpretation of this subchapter, except to the extent that such construction is inconsistent with the specific requirements of this chapter.

§ 949p–2.   Pretrial conference

(a) MOTION. — At any time after service of charges, any party may move for a pretrial conference to consider matters relating to classified information that may arise in connection with the prosecution.

(b) CONFERENCE. — Following a motion under subsection (a), or sua sponte, the military judge shall promptly hold a pretrial conference. Upon request by either party, the court shall hold such conference ex parte to the extent necessary to protect classified information from disclosure, in accordance with the practice of the Federal courts under the Classified Information Procedures Act (18 U.S.C. App.).

(c) MATTERS TO BE ESTABLISHED AT PRETRIAL CONFERENCE. —

(1) TIMING OF SUBSEQUENT ACTIONS. — At the pretrial conference, the military judge shall establish the timing of —

(A) requests for discovery;

(B) the provision of notice required by section 949p–5 of this title; and

(C) the initiation of the procedure established by section 949p–6 of this title.

(2) OTHER MATTERS. — At the pretrial conference, the military judge may also consider any matter —

(A) which relates to classified information; or

(B) which may promote a fair and expeditious trial.

(d) EFFECT OF ADMISSIONS BY ACCUSED AT PRETRIAL CONFERENCE. — No admission made by the accused or by any counsel for the accused at a pretrial conference under this section may be used against the accused unless the admission is in writing and is signed by the accused and by the counsel for the accused.

§ 949p–3. Protective orders

Upon motion of the trial counsel, the military judge shall issue an order to protect against the disclosure of any classified information that has been disclosed by the United States to any accused in any military commission under this chapter or that has otherwise been provided to, or obtained by, any such accused in any such military commission.

§ 949p–4. Discovery of, and access to, classified information by the accused

(a) LIMITATIONS ON DISCOVERY OR ACCESS BY THE ACCUSED. —

(1) DECLARATIONS BY THE UNITED STATES OF DAMAGE TO NATIONAL SECURITY. — In any case before a military commission in which the United States seeks to delete, withhold, or otherwise obtain other relief with respect to the discovery of or access to any classified information, the trial counsel shall submit a declaration invoking the United States' classified information privilege and setting forth the damage to the national security that the discovery of or access to such information reasonably could be expected to cause. The declaration shall be signed by a knowledgeable United States official possessing authority to classify information.

(2) STANDARD FOR AUTHORIZATION OF DISCOVERY OR ACCESS. — Upon the submission of a declaration under paragraph (1), the military judge may not authorize the discovery of or access to such classified information unless the military judge determines that such classified information would be noncumulative, relevant, and helpful to a legally cognizable defense, rebuttal of the prosecution's case, or to sentencing, in accordance with standards generally applicable to discovery of or access to classified information in Federal criminal cases.

If the discovery of or access to such classified information is authorized, it shall be addressed in accordance with the requirements of subsection (b).

(b) DISCOVERY OF CLASSIFIED INFORMATION. —

(1) SUBSTITUTIONS AND OTHER RELIEF. — The military judge, in assessing the accused's discovery of or access to classified information under this section, may authorize the United States —

(A) to delete or withhold specified items of classified information;

(B) to substitute a summary for classified information; or

(C) to substitute a statement admitting relevant facts that the classified information or material would tend to prove.

(2) EX PARTE PRESENTATIONS. — The military judge shall permit the trial counsel to make a request for an authorization under paragraph (1) in the form of an ex parte presentation to the extent necessary to protect classified information, in accordance with the practice of the Federal courts under the Classified Information Procedures Act (18 U.S.C. App.). If the military judge enters an order granting relief following such an ex parte showing, the entire presentation (including the text of any written submission, verbatim transcript of the ex parte oral conference or hearing, and any exhibits received by the court as part of the ex parte presentation) shall be sealed and preserved in the records of the military commission to be made available to the appellate court in the event of an appeal.

(3) ACTION BY MILITARY JUDGE. — The military judge shall grant the request of the trial counsel to substitute a summary or to substitute a statement admitting relevant facts, or to provide other relief in accordance with paragraph (1), if the military judge finds that the summary, statement, or other relief would provide the accused with substantially the same ability to make a defense as would discovery of or access to the specific classified information.

(c) RECONSIDERATION. — An order of a military judge authorizing a request of the trial counsel to substitute, summarize, withhold, or prevent access to classified information under this section is not subject to a motion for reconsideration by the accused, if such order was entered pursuant to an ex parte showing under this section.

§ 949p–5. Notice by accused of intention to disclose classified information

(a) NOTICE BY ACCUSED. —

(1) NOTIFICATION OF TRIAL COUNSEL AND MILITARY JUDGE. — If an accused reasonably expects to disclose, or to cause the disclosure of, classified information in any manner in connection with any trial or pretrial proceeding involving the prosecution of such accused, the accused shall, within the time specified by the military judge or, where no time is specified, within 30 days before trial, notify the trial counsel and the military judge in writing. Such notice shall include a brief description of the classified information. Whenever the accused learns of additional classified information the accused reasonably expects to disclose, or to cause the disclosure of, at any such

proceeding, the accused shall notify trial counsel and the military judge in writing as soon as possible thereafter and shall include a brief description of the classified information.

(2) LIMITATION ON DISCLOSURE BY ACCUSED. — No accused shall disclose, or cause the disclosure of, any information known or believed to be classified in connection with a trial or pretrial proceeding until —

(A) notice has been given under paragraph (1); and

(B) the United States has been afforded a reasonable opportunity to seek a determination pursuant to the procedure set forth in section 949p–6 of this title and the time for the United States to appeal such determination under section 950d of this title has expired or any appeal under that section by the United States is decided.

(b) FAILURE TO COMPLY. — If the accused fails to comply with the requirements of subsection (a), the military judge —

(1) may preclude disclosure of any classified information not made the subject of notification; and

(2) may prohibit the examination by the accused of any witness with respect to any such information.

§ 949p–6. Procedure for cases involving classified information

(a) MOTION FOR HEARING. —

(1) REQUEST FOR HEARING. — Within the time specified by the military judge for the filing of a motion under this section, either party may request the military judge to conduct a hearing to make all determinations concerning the use, relevance, or admissibility of classified information that would otherwise be made during the trial or pretrial proceeding.

(2) CONDUCT OF HEARING. — Upon a request by either party under paragraph (1), the military judge shall conduct such a hearing and shall rule prior to conducting any further proceedings.

(3) IN CAMERA HEARING UPON DECLARATION TO COURT BY APPROPRIATE OFFICIAL OF RISK OF DISCLOSURE OF CLASSI-FIED INFORMATION. — Any hearing held pursuant to this subsection (or any portion of such hearing specified in the request of a knowledgeable United States official) shall be held in camera if a knowledgeable United States official possessing authority to classify information submits to the military judge a declaration that a public proceeding may result in the disclosure of classified information. Classified information is not subject to disclosure under this section unless the information is relevant and necessary to an element of the offense or a legally cognizable defense and is otherwise admissible in evidence.

(4) MILITARY JUDGE TO MAKE DETERMINATIONS IN WRITING. — As to each item of classified information, the military judge shall set forth in writing the basis for the determination.

(b) NOTICE AND USE OF CLASSIFIED INFORMATION BY THE

GOVERNMENT. —

(1) NOTICE TO ACCUSED. — Before any hearing is conducted pursuant to a request by the trial counsel under subsection (a), trial counsel shall provide the accused with notice of the classified information that is at issue. Such notice shall identify the specific classified information at issue whenever that information previously has been made available to the accused by the United States. When the United States has not previously made the information available to the accused in connection with the case the information may be described by generic category, in such forms as the military judge may approve, rather than by identification of the specific information of concern to the United States.

(2) ORDER BY MILITARY JUDGE UPON REQUEST OF ACCUSED. — Whenever the trial counsel requests a hearing under subsection (a), the military judge, upon request of the accused, may order the trial counsel to provide the accused, prior to trial, such details as to the portion of the charge or specification at issue in the hearing as are needed to give the accused fair notice to prepare for the hearing.

(c) SUBSTITUTIONS. —

(1) IN CAMERA PRETRIAL HEARING. — Upon request of the trial counsel pursuant to the Military Commission Rules of Evidence, and in accordance with the security procedures established by the military judge, the military judge shall conduct a classified in camera pretrial hearing concerning the admissibility of classified information.

(2) PROTECTION OF SOURCES, METHODS, AND ACTIVITIES BY WHICH EVIDENCE ACQUIRED. — When trial counsel seeks to introduce evidence before a military commission under this chapter and the Executive branch has classified the sources, methods, or activities by which the United States acquired the evidence, the military judge shall permit trial counsel to introduce the evidence, including a substituted evidentiary foundation pursuant to the procedures described in subsection (d), while protecting from disclosure information identifying those sources, methods, or activities, if —

(A) the evidence is otherwise admissible; and

(B) the military judge finds that —

(i) the evidence is reliable; and

(ii) the redaction is consistent with affording the accused a fair trial.

(d) ALTERNATIVE PROCEDURE FOR DISCLOSURE OF CLASSIFIED INFORMATION. —

(1) MOTION BY THE UNITED STATES. — Upon any determination by the military judge authorizing the disclosure of specific classified information under the procedures established by this section, the trial counsel may move that, in lieu of the disclosure of such specific classified information, the military judge order —

(A) the substitution for such classified information of a statement admitting relevant facts that the specific classified information would tend to prove;

(B) the substitution for such classified information of a summary of the specific classified information; or

(C) any other procedure or redaction limiting the disclosure of specific classified information.

(2) ACTION ON MOTION. — The military judge shall grant such a motion of the trial counsel if the military judge finds that the statement, summary, or other procedure or redaction will provide the defendant with substantially the same ability to make his defense as would disclosure of the specific classified information.

(3) HEARING ON MOTION. — The military judge shall hold a hearing on any motion under this subsection. Any such hearing shall be held in camera at the request of a knowledgeable United States official possessing authority to classify information.

(4) SUBMISSION OF STATEMENT OF DAMAGE TO NATIONAL SECURITY IF DISCLOSURE ORDERED. — The trial counsel may, in connection with a motion under paragraph (1), submit to the military judge a declaration signed by a knowledgeable United States official possessing authority to classify information certifying that disclosure of classified information would cause identifiable damage to the national security of the United States and explaining the basis for the classification of such information. If so requested by the trial counsel, the military judge shall examine such declaration during an ex parte presentation.

(e) SEALING OF RECORDS OF IN CAMERA HEARINGS. — If at the close of an in camera hearing under this section (or any portion of a hearing under this section that is held in camera), the military judge determines that the classified information at issue may not be disclosed or elicited at the trial or pretrial proceeding, the record of such in camera hearing shall be sealed and preserved for use in the event of an appeal. The accused may seek reconsideration of the military judge's determination prior to or during trial.

(f) PROHIBITION ON DISCLOSURE OF CLASSIFIED INFORMATION BY THE ACCUSED; RELIEF FOR ACCUSED WHEN THE UNITED STATES OPPOSES DISCLOSURE. —

(1) ORDER TO PREVENT DISCLOSURE BY ACCUSED. — Whenever the military judge denies a motion by the trial counsel that the judge issue an order under subsection (a), (c), or (d) and the trial counsel files with the military judge a declaration signed by a knowledgeable United States official possessing authority to classify information objecting to disclosure of the classified information at issue, the military judge shall order that the accused not disclose or cause the disclosure of such information.

(2) RESULT OF ORDER UNDER PARAGRAPH (1). — Whenever an accused is prevented by an order under paragraph (1) from disclosing or

causing the disclosure of classified information, the military judge shall dismiss the case, except that, when the military judge determines that the interests of justice would not be served by dismissal of the case, the military judge shall order such other action, in lieu of dismissing the charge or specification, as the military judge determines is appropriate.

Such action may include, but need not be limited to, the following:

(A) Dismissing specified charges or specifications.

(B) Finding against the United States on any issue as to which the excluded classified information relates.

(C) Striking or precluding all or part of the testimony of a witness.

(3) TIME FOR THE UNITED STATES TO SEEK INTERLOCUTORY APPEAL. — An order under paragraph (2) shall not take effect until the military judge has afforded the United States —

(A) an opportunity to appeal such order under section 950d of this title; and

(B) an opportunity thereafter to withdraw its objection to the disclosure of the classified information at issue.

(g) RECIPROCITY. —

(1) DISCLOSURE OF REBUTTAL INFORMATION. — Whenever the military judge determines that classified information may be disclosed in connection with a trial or pretrial proceeding, the military judge shall, unless the interests of fairness do not so require, order the United States to provide the accused with the information it expects to use to rebut the classified information. The military judge may place the United States under a continuing duty to disclose such rebuttal information.

(2) SANCTION FOR FAILURE TO COMPLY. — If the United States fails to comply with its obligation under this subsection, the military judge —

(A) may exclude any evidence not made the subject of a required disclosure; and

(B) may prohibit the examination by the United States of any witness with respect to such information.

§ 949p–7. Introduction of classified information into evidence

(a) PRESERVATION OF CLASSIFICATION STATUS. — Writings, recordings, and photographs containing classified information may be admitted into evidence in proceedings of military commissions under this chapter without change in their classification status.

(b) PRECAUTIONS BY MILITARY JUDGES. —

(1) PRECAUTIONS IN ADMITTING CLASSIFIED INFORMATION INTO EVIDENCE. — The military judge in a trial by military commission, in order to prevent unnecessary disclosure of classified information, may order

admission into evidence of only part of a writing, recording, or photograph, or may order admission into evidence of the whole writing, recording, or photograph with excision of some or all of the classified information contained therein, unless the whole ought in fairness be considered.

(2) CLASSIFIED INFORMATION KEPT UNDER SEAL. — The military judge shall allow classified information offered or accepted into evidence to remain under seal during the trial, even if such evidence is disclosed in the military commission, and may, upon motion by the United States, seal exhibits containing classified information for any period after trial as necessary to prevent a disclosure of classified information when a knowledgeable United States official possessing authority to classify information submits to the military judge a declaration setting forth the damage to the national security that the disclosure of such information reasonably could be expected to cause.

(c) TAKING OF TESTIMONY. —

(1) OBJECTION BY TRIAL COUNSEL. — During the examination of a witness, trial counsel may object to any question or line of inquiry that may require the witness to disclose classified information not previously found to be admissible.

(2) ACTION BY MILITARY JUDGE. — Following an objection under paragraph (1), the military judge shall take such suitable action to determine whether the response is admissible as will safeguard against the compromise of any classified information. Such action may include requiring trial counsel to provide the military judge with a proffer of the witness" response to the question or line of inquiry and requiring the accused to provide the military judge with a proffer of the nature of the information sought to be elicited by the accused. Upon request, the military judge may accept an ex parte proffer by trial counsel to the extent necessary to protect classified information from disclosure, in accordance with the practice of the Federal courts under the Classified Information Procedures Act (18 U.S.C. App.).

(d) DISCLOSURE AT TRIAL OF CERTAIN STATEMENTS PREVIOUSLY MADE BY A WITNESS. —

(1) MOTION FOR PRODUCTION OF STATEMENTS IN POSSESSION OF THE UNITED STATES. — After a witness called by the trial counsel has testified on direct examination, the military judge, on motion of the accused, may order production of statements of the witness in the possession of the United States which relate to the subject matter as to which the witness has testified. This paragraph does not preclude discovery or assertion of a privilege otherwise authorized.

(2) INVOCATION OF PRIVILEGE BY THE UNITED STATES. — If the United States invokes a privilege, the trial counsel may provide the prior statements of the witness to the military judge during an ex parte presentation to the extent necessary to protect classified information from disclosure, in accordance with the practice of the Federal courts under the Classified Information Procedures Act (18 U.S.C. App.).

(3) ACTION BY MILITARY JUDGE ON MOTION. — If the military judge finds that disclosure of any portion of the statement identified by the United States as classified would be detrimental to the national security in the degree to warrant classification under the applicable Executive Order, statute, or regulation, that such portion of the statement is consistent with the testimony of the witness, and that the disclosure of such portion is not necessary to afford the accused a fair trial, the military judge shall excise that portion from the statement. If the military judge finds that such portion of the statement is inconsistent with the testimony of the witness or that its disclosure is necessary to afford the accused a fair trial, the military judge, shall, upon the request of the trial counsel, review alternatives to disclosure in accordance with section 949p–6(d) of this title.

SUBCHAPTER VI. SENTENCES

§ 949s. Cruel or unusual punishments prohibited

Punishment by flogging, or by branding, marking, or tattooing on the body, or any other cruel or unusual punishment, may not be adjudged by a military commission under this chapter or inflicted under this chapter upon any person subject to this chapter. The use of irons, single or double, except for the purpose of safe custody, is prohibited under this chapter.

§ 949t. Maximum limits

The punishment which a military commission under this chapter may direct for an offense may not exceed such limits as the President or Secretary of Defense may prescribe for that offense.

§ 949u. Execution of confinement

(a) IN GENERAL. — Under such regulations as the Secretary of Defense may prescribe, a sentence of confinement adjudged by a military commission under this chapter may be carried into execution by confinement —

(1) in any place of confinement under the control of any of the armed forces; or

(2) in any penal or correctional institution under the control of the United States or its allies, or which the United States may be allowed to use.

(b) TREATMENT DURING CONFINEMENT BY OTHER THAN THE ARMED FORCES. — Persons confined under subsection (a)(2) in a penal or correctional institution not under the control of an armed force are subject to the same discipline and treatment as persons confined or committed by the courts of the United States or of the State, District of Columbia, or place in which the institution is situated.

SUBCHAPTER VII.   POST-TRIAL PROCEDURE AND REVIEW OF MILITARY COMMISSIONS

§ 950a.   Error of law; lesser included offense

(a) ERROR OF LAW. — A finding or sentence of a military commission under this chapter may not be held incorrect on the ground of an error of law unless the error materially prejudices the substantial rights of the accused.

(b) LESSER INCLUDED OFFENSE. — Any reviewing authority with the power to approve or affirm a finding of guilty by a military commission under this chapter may approve or affirm, instead, so much of the finding as includes a lesser included offense.

§ 950b.   Review by the convening authority

(a) NOTICE TO CONVENING AUTHORITY OF FINDINGS AND SENTENCE. — The findings and sentence of a military commission under this chapter shall be reported in writing promptly to the convening authority after the announcement of the sentence.

(b) SUBMITTAL OF MATTERS BY ACCUSED TO CONVENING AUTHORITY. —

(1) The accused may submit to the convening authority matters for consideration by the convening authority with respect to the findings and the sentence of the military commission under this chapter.

(2) (A) Except as provided in subparagraph (B), a submittal under paragraph (1) shall be made in writing within 20 days after the accused has been give an authenticated record of trial under section 949o(c) of this title.

(B) If the accused shows that additional time is required for the accused to make a submittal under paragraph (1), the convening authority may, for good cause, extend the applicable period under subparagraph (A) for not more than an additional 20 days.

(3) The accused may waive the accused's right to make a submittal to the convening authority under paragraph (1). Such a waiver shall be made in writing, and may not be revoked. For the purposes of subsection (c)(2), the time within which the accused may make a submittal under this subsection shall be deemed to have expired upon the submittal of a waiver under this paragraph to the convening authority.

(c) ACTION BY CONVENING AUTHORITY. —

(1) The authority under this subsection to modify the findings and sentence of a military commission under this chapter is a matter of the sole discretion and prerogative of the convening authority.

(2) The convening authority is not required to take action on the findings of a military commission under this chapter. If the convening authority takes action on the findings, the convening authority may, in the sole discretion of the convening authority, only —

(A) dismiss any charge or specification by setting aside a finding of guilty thereto; or

(B) change a finding of guilty to a charge to a finding of guilty to an offense that is a lesser included offense of the offense stated in the charge.

(3) (A) The convening authority shall take action on the sentence of a military commission under this chapter.

(B) Subject to regulations prescribed by the Secretary of Defense, action under this paragraph may be taken only after consideration of any matters submitted by the accused under subsection (b) or after the time for submitting such matters expires, whichever is earlier.

(C) In taking action under this paragraph, the convening authority may, in the sole discretion of the convening authority, approve, disapprove, commute, or suspend the sentence in whole or in part. The convening authority may not increase a sentence beyond that which is found by the military commission.

(4) The convening authority shall serve on the accused or on defense counsel notice of any action taken by the convening authority under this subsection.

(d) ORDER OF REVISION OR REHEARING. —

(1) Subject to paragraphs (2) and (3), the convening authority of a military commission under this chapter may, in the sole discretion of the convening authority, order a proceeding in revision or a rehearing.

(2) (A) Except as provided in subparagraph (B), a proceeding in revision may be ordered by the convening authority if —

(i) there is an apparent error or omission in the record; or

(ii) the record shows improper or inconsistent action by the military commission with respect to the findings or sentence that can be rectified without material prejudice to the substantial rights of the accused.

(B) In no case may a proceeding in revision —

(i) reconsider a finding of not guilty of a specification or a ruling which amounts to a finding of not guilty;

(ii) reconsider a finding of not guilty of any charge, unless there has been a finding of guilty under a specification laid under that charge, which sufficiently alleges a violation; or

(iii) increase the severity of the sentence unless the sentence prescribed for the offense is mandatory.

(3) A rehearing may be ordered by the convening authority if the convening authority disapproves the findings and sentence and states the reasons for disapproval of the findings. If the convening authority disapproves the finding and sentence and does not order a rehearing, the convening authority shall dismiss the charges. A rehearing as to the findings may not be ordered by the convening authority when there is a lack of sufficient evidence in the record to

support the findings. A rehearing as to the sentence may be ordered by the convening authority if the convening authority disapproves the sentence.

§ 950c.   Appellate referral; waiver or withdrawal of appeal

(a) AUTOMATIC REFERRAL FOR APPELLATE REVIEW. — Except as provided in subsection (b), in each case in which the final decision of a military commission under this chapter (as approved by the convening authority) includes a finding of guilty, the convening authority shall refer the case to the United States Court of Military Commission Review. Any such referral shall be made in accordance with procedures prescribed under regulations of the Secretary.

(b) WAIVER OF RIGHT OF REVIEW. —

(1) Except in a case in which the sentence as approved under section 950b of this title extends to death, an accused may file with the convening authority a statement expressly waiving the right of the accused to appellate review by the United States Court of Military Commission Review under section 950f of this title of the final decision of the military commission under this chapter.

(2) A waiver under paragraph (1) shall be signed by both the accused and a defense counsel.

(3) A waiver under paragraph (1) must be filed, if at all, within 10 days after notice of the action is served on the accused or on defense counsel under section 950b(c)(4) of this title. The convening authority, for good cause, may extend the period for such filing by not more than 30 days.

(c) WITHDRAWAL OF APPEAL. — Except in a case in which the sentence as approved under section 950b of this title extends to death, the accused may withdraw an appeal at any time.

(d) EFFECT OF WAIVER OR WITHDRAWAL. — A waiver of the right to appellate review or the withdrawal of an appeal under this section bars review under section 950f of this title.

§ 950d.   Interlocutory appeals by the United States

(a) INTERLOCUTORY APPEAL. — Except as provided in subsection (b), in a trial by military commission under this chapter, the United States may take an interlocutory appeal to the United States Court of Military Commission Review of any order or ruling of the military judge —

(1) that terminates proceedings of the military commission with respect to a charge or specification;

(2) that excludes evidence that is substantial proof of a fact material in the proceeding;

(3) that relates to a matter under subsection (c) or (d) of section 949d of this title; or

(4) that, with respect to classified information —

(A) authorizes the disclosure of such information;

(B) imposes sanctions for nondisclosure of such information; or

(C) refuses a protective order sought by the United States to prevent the disclosure of such information.

(b) LIMITATION. — The United States may not appeal under subsection (a) an order or ruling that is, or amounts to, a finding of not guilty by the military commission with respect to a charge or specification.

(c) SCOPE OF APPEAL RIGHT WITH RESPECT TO CLASSIFIED INFORMATION. — The United States has the right to appeal under paragraph (4) of subsection (a) whenever the military judge enters an order or ruling that would require the disclosure of classified information, without regard to whether the order or ruling appealed from was entered under this chapter, another provision of law, a rule, or otherwise. Any such appeal may embrace any preceding order, ruling, or reasoning constituting the basis of the order or ruling that would authorize such disclosure.

(d) TIMING AND ACTION ON INTERLOCUTORY APPEALS RELATING TO CLASSIFIED INFORMATION. —

(1) APPEAL TO BE EXPEDITED. — An appeal taken pursuant to paragraph (4) of subsection (a) shall be expedited by the United States Court of Military Commission Review.

(2) APPEALS BEFORE TRIAL. — If such an appeal is taken before trial, the appeal shall be taken within 10 days after the order or ruling from which the appeal is made and the trial shall not commence until the appeal is decided.

(3) APPEALS DURING TRIAL. — If such an appeal is taken during trial, the military judge shall adjourn the trial until the appeal is decided, and the court of appeals —

(A) shall hear argument on such appeal within 4 days of the adjournment of the trial (excluding weekends and holidays);

(B) may dispense with written briefs other than the supporting materials previously submitted to the military judge;

(C) shall render its decision within four days of argument on appeal (excluding weekends and holidays); and

(D) may dispense with the issuance of a written opinion in rendering its decision.

(e) NOTICE AND TIMING OF OTHER APPEALS. — The United States shall take an appeal of an order or ruling under subsection (a), other than an appeal under paragraph (4) of that subsection, by filing a notice of appeal with the military judge within 5 days after the date of the order or ruling.

(f) METHOD OF APPEAL. — An appeal under this section shall be forwarded, by means specified in regulations prescribed by the Secretary of Defense, directly to the United States Court of Military Commission Review.

(g) APPEALS COURT TO ACT ONLY WITH RESPECT TO MATTER OF

LAW. — In ruling on an appeal under paragraph (1), (2), or (3) of subsection (a), the appeals court may act only with respect to matters of law.

(h) SUBSEQUENT APPEAL RIGHTS OF ACCUSED NOT AFFECTED. — An appeal under paragraph (4) of subsection (a), and a decision on such appeal, shall not affect the right of the accused, in a subsequent appeal from a judgment of conviction, to claim as error reversal by the military judge on remand of a ruling appealed from during trial.

§ 950e.   Rehearings

(a) COMPOSITION OF MILITARY COMMISSION FOR REHEARING. — Each rehearing under this chapter shall take place before a military commission under this chapter composed of members who were not members of the military commission which first heard the case.

(b) SCOPE OF REHEARING. —

(1) Upon a rehearing —

(A) the accused may not be tried for any offense of which the accused was found not guilty by the first military commission; and

(B) no sentence in excess of or more than the original sentence may be imposed unless —

(i) the sentence is based upon a finding of guilty of an offense not considered upon the merits in the original proceedings; or

(ii) the sentence prescribed for the offense is mandatory.

(2) Upon a rehearing, if the sentence approved after the first military commission was in accordance with a pretrial agreement and the accused at the rehearing changes his plea with respect to the charges or specifications upon which the pretrial agreement was based, or otherwise does not comply with pretrial agreement, the sentence as to those charges or specifications may include any punishment not in excess of that lawfully adjudged at the first military commission.

§ 950f.   Review by United States Court of Military Commission Review

(a) ESTABLISHMENT. — There is a court of record to be known as the "United States Court of Military Commission Review" (in this section referred to as the "Court"). The Court shall consist of one or more panels, each composed of not less than three appellate military judges. For the purpose of reviewing decisions of military commissions under this chapter, the Court may sit in panels or as a whole, in accordance with rules prescribed by the Secretary of Defense.

(b) JUDGES. —

(1) Judges on the Court shall be assigned or appointed in a manner consistent with the provisions of this subsection.

(2) The Secretary of Defense may assign persons who are appellate military judges to be judges on the Court. Any judge so assigned shall be a

commissioned officer of the armed forces, and shall meet the qualifications for military judges prescribed by section 948j(b) of this title.

(3) The President may appoint, by and with the advice and consent of the Senate, additional judges to the United States Court of Military Commission Review.

(4) No person may serve as a judge on the Court in any case in which that person acted as a military judge, counsel, or reviewing official.

(c) CASES TO BE REVIEWED. — The Court shall, in accordance with procedures prescribed under regulations of the Secretary, review the record in each case that is referred to the Court by the convening authority under section 950c of this title with respect to any matter properly raised by the accused.

(d) STANDARD AND SCOPE OF REVIEW. — In a case reviewed by the Court under this section, the Court may act only with respect to the findings and sentence as approved by the convening authority. The Court may affirm only such findings of guilty, and the sentence or such part or amount of the sentence, as the Court finds correct in law and fact and determines, on the basis of the entire record, should be approved. In considering the record, the Court may weigh the evidence, judge the credibility of witnesses, and determine controverted questions of fact, recognizing that the military commission saw and heard the witnesses.

(e) REHEARINGS. — If the Court sets aside the findings or sentence, the Court may, except where the setting aside is based on lack of sufficient evidence in the record to support the findings, order a rehearing. If the Court sets aside the findings or sentence and does not order a rehearing, the Court shall order that the charges be dismissed.

§ 950g. Review by United States Court of Appeals for the District of Columbia Circuit; writ of certiorari to Supreme Court

(a) EXCLUSIVE APPELLATE JURISDICTION. — Except as provided in subsection (b), the United States Court of Appeals for the District of Columbia Circuit shall have exclusive jurisdiction to determine the validity of a final judgment rendered by a military commission (as approved by the convening authority and, where applicable, the United States Court of Military Commission Review) under this chapter.

(b) EXHAUSTION OF OTHER APPEALS. — The United States Court of Appeals for the District of Columbia Circuit may not review a final judgment described in subsection (a) until all other appeals under this chapter have been waived or exhausted.

(c) TIME FOR SEEKING REVIEW. — A petition for review by the United States Court of Appeals for the District of Columbia Circuit must be filed by the accused in the Court of Appeals not later than 20 days after the date on which —

(1) written notice of the final decision of the United States Court of Military Commission Review is served on the accused or on defense counsel; or

(2) the accused submits, in the form prescribed by section 950c of this title,

a written notice waiving the right of the accused to review by the United States Court of Military Commission Review.

(d) SCOPE AND NATURE OF REVIEW. — The United States Court of Appeals for the District of Columbia Circuit may act under this section only with respect to the findings and sentence as approved by the convening authority and as affirmed or set aside as incorrect in law by the United States Court of Military Commission Review, and shall take action only with respect to matters of law, including the sufficiency of the evidence to support the verdict.

(e) REVIEW BY SUPREME COURT. — The Supreme Court may review by writ of certiorari pursuant to section 1254 of title 28 the final judgment of the United States Court of Appeals for the District of Columbia Circuit under this section.

§ 950h. Appellate counsel

(a) APPOINTMENT. — The Secretary of Defense shall, by regulation, establish procedures for the appointment of appellate counsel for the United States and for the accused in military commissions under this chapter. Appellate counsel shall meet the qualifications of counsel for appearing before military commissions under this chapter.

(b) REPRESENTATION OF UNITED STATES. — Appellate counsel appointed under subsection (a) —

(1) shall represent the United States in any appeal or review proceeding under this chapter before the United States Court of Military Commission Review; and

(2) may, when requested to do so by the Attorney General in a case arising under this chapter, represent the United States before the United States Court of Appeals for the District of Columbia Circuit or the Supreme Court.

(c) REPRESENTATION OF ACCUSED. — The accused shall be represented by appellate counsel appointed under subsection (a) before the United States Court of Military Commission Review, the United States Court of Appeals for the District of Columbia Circuit, and the Supreme Court, and by civilian counsel if retained by the accused. Any such civilian counsel shall meet the qualifications under paragraph (3) of section 949c(b) of this title for civilian counsel appearing before military commissions under this chapter and shall be subject to the requirements of paragraph (7) of that section.

§ 950i. Execution of sentence; suspension of sentence

(a) IN GENERAL. — The Secretary of Defense is authorized to carry out a sentence imposed by a military commission under this chapter in accordance with such procedures as the Secretary may prescribe.

(b) EXECUTION OF SENTENCE OF DEATH ONLY UPON APPROVAL BY THE PRESIDENT. — If the sentence of a military commission under this chapter extends to death, that part of the sentence providing for death may not be executed until approved by the President. In such a case, the President may commute, remit, or suspend the sentence, or any part thereof, as he sees fit.

(c) EXECUTION OF SENTENCE OF DEATH ONLY UPON FINAL JUDGMENT OF LEGALITY OF PROCEEDINGS. —

(1) If the sentence of a military commission under this chapter extends to death, the sentence may not be executed until there is a final judgment as to the legality of the proceedings (and with respect to death, approval under subsection (b)).

(2) A judgment as to legality of proceedings is final for purposes of paragraph (1) when review is completed in accordance with the judgment of the United States Court of Military Commission Review and —

(A) the time for the accused to file a petition for review by the United States Court of Appeals for the District of Columbia Circuit has expired, the accused has not filed a timely petition for such review, and the case is not otherwise under review by the Court of Appeals; or

(B) review is completed in accordance with the judgment of the United States Court of Appeals for the District of Columbia Circuit and —

(i) a petition for a writ of certiorari is not timely filed;

(ii) such a petition is denied by the Supreme Court; or

(iii) review is otherwise completed in accordance with the judgment of the Supreme Court.

(d) SUSPENSION OF SENTENCE. — The Secretary of the Defense, or the convening authority acting on the case (if other than the Secretary), may suspend the execution of any sentence or part thereof in the case, except a sentence of death.

§ 950j.   Finality of proceedings, findings, and sentences

The appellate review of records of trial provided by this chapter, and the proceedings, findings, and sentences of military commissions as approved, reviewed, or affirmed as required by this chapter, are final and conclusive. Orders publishing the proceedings of military commissions under this chapter are binding upon all departments, courts, agencies, and officers of the United States, subject only to action by the Secretary or the convening authority as provided in section 950i(c) of this title and the authority of the President.

SUBCHAPTER VIII.   PUNITIVE MATTERS

§ 950p.   Definitions; construction of certain offenses; common circumstances

(a) DEFINITIONS. — In this subchapter:

(1) The term "military objective" means combatants and those objects during hostilities which, by their nature, location, purpose, or use, effectively contribute to the war-fighting or war-sustaining capability of an opposing force and whose total or partial destruction, capture, or neutralization would constitute a definite military advantage to the attacker under the circum-

stances at the time of an attack.

(2) The term "protected person" means any person entitled to protection under one or more of the Geneva Conventions, including civilians not taking an active part in hostilities, military personnel placed out of combat by sickness, wounds, or detention, and military medical or religious personnel. (3) The term "protected property" means any property specifically protected by the law of war, including buildings dedicated to religion, education, art, science, or charitable purposes, historic monuments, hospitals, and places where the sick and wounded are collected, but only if and to the extent such property is not being used for military purposes or is not otherwise a military objective. The term includes objects properly identified by one of the distinctive emblems of the Geneva Conventions, but does not include civilian property that is a military objective.

(b) CONSTRUCTION OF CERTAIN OFFENSES. — The intent required for offenses under paragraphs (1), (2), (3), (4), and (12) of section 950t of this title precludes the applicability of such offenses with regard to collateral damage or to death, damage, or injury incident to a lawful attack.

(c) COMMON CIRCUMSTANCES. — An offense specified in this subchapter is triable by military commission under this chapter only if the offense is committed in the context of and associated with hostilities.

(d) EFFECT. — The provisions of this subchapter codify offenses that have traditionally been triable by military commission. This chapter does not establish new crimes that did not exist before the date of the enactment of this subchapter, as amended by the National Defense Authorization Act for Fiscal Year 2010, but rather codifies those crimes for trial by military commission. Because the provisions of this subchapter codify offenses that have traditionally been triable under the law of war or otherwise triable by military commission, this subchapter does not preclude trial for offenses that occurred before the date of the enactment of this subchapter, as so amended.

§ 950q. Principals

Any person punishable under this chapter who —

(1) commits an offense punishable by this chapter, or aids, abets, counsels, commands, or procures its commission;

(2) causes an act to be done which if directly performed by him would be punishable by this chapter; or

(3) is a superior commander who, with regard to acts punishable by this chapter, knew, had reason to know, or should have known, that a subordinate was about to commit such acts or had done so and who failed to take the necessary and reasonable measures to prevent such acts or to punish the perpetrators thereof, is a principal.

§ 950r. Accessory after the fact

Any person subject to this chapter who, knowing that an offense punishable by this chapter has been committed, receives, comforts, or assists the offender in order to hinder or prevent his apprehension, trial, or punishment shall be punished as a military commission under this chapter may direct.

§ 950s.   Conviction of lesser offenses

An accused may be found guilty of an offense necessarily included in the offense charged or of an attempt to commit either the offense charged or an attempt to commit either the offense charged or an offense necessarily included therein.

§ 950t.   Crimes triable by military commission

The following offenses shall be triable by military commission under this chapter at any time without limitation:

(1) MURDER OF PROTECTED PERSONS. — Any person subject to this chapter who intentionally kills one or more protected persons shall be punished by death or such other punishment as a military commission under this chapter may direct.

(2) ATTACKING CIVILIANS. — Any person subject to this chapter who intentionally engages in an attack upon a civilian population as such, or individual civilians not taking active part in hostilities, shall be punished, if death results to one or more of the victims, by death or such other punishment as a military commission under this chapter may direct, and, if death does not result to any of the victims, by such punishment, other than death, as a military commission under this chapter may direct.

(3) ATTACKING CIVILIAN OBJECTS. — Any person subject to this chapter who intentionally engages in an attack upon a civilian object that is not a military objective shall be punished as a military commission under this chapter may direct.

(4) ATTACKING PROTECTED PROPERTY. — Any person subject to this chapter who intentionally engages in an attack upon protected property shall be punished as a military commission under this chapter may direct.

(5) PILLAGING. — Any person subject to this chapter who intentionally and in the absence of military necessity appropriates or seizes property for private or personal use, without the consent of a person with authority to permit such appropriation or seizure, shall be punished as a military commission under this chapter may direct.

(6) DENYING QUARTER. — Any person subject to this chapter who, with effective command or control over subordinate groups, declares, orders, or otherwise indicates to those groups that there shall be no survivors or surrender accepted, with the intent to threaten an adversary or to conduct hostilities such that there would be no survivors or surrender accepted, shall be punished as a military commission under this chapter may direct.

(7) TAKING HOSTAGES. — Any person subject to this chapter who, having knowingly seized or detained one or more persons, threatens to kill, injure, or continue to detain such person or persons with the intent of compelling any nation, person other than the hostage, or group of persons to act or refrain

from acting as an explicit or implicit condition for the safety or release of such person or persons, shall be punished, if death results to one or more of the victims, by death or such other punishment as a military commission under this chapter may direct, and, if death does not result to any of the victims, by such punishment, other than death, as a military commission under this chapter may direct.

(8) EMPLOYING POISON OR SIMILAR WEAPONS. — Any person subject to this chapter who intentionally, as a method of warfare, employs a substance or weapon that releases a substance that causes death or serious and lasting damage to health in the ordinary course of events, through its asphyxiating, bacteriological, or toxic properties, shall be punished, if death results to one or more of the victims, by death or such other punishment as a military commission under this chapter may direct, and, if death does not result to any of the victims, by such punishment, other than death, as a military commission under this chapter may direct.

(9) USING PROTECTED PERSONS AS A SHIELD. — Any person subject to this chapter who positions, or otherwise takes advantage of, a protected person with the intent to shield a military objective from attack. or to shield, favor, or impede military operations, shall be punished, if death results to one or more of the victims, by death or such other punishment as a military commission under this chapter may direct, and, if death does not result to any of the victims, by such punishment, other than death, as a military commission under this chapter may direct.

(10) USING PROTECTED PROPERTY AS A SHIELD. — Any person subject to this chapter who positions, or otherwise takes advantage of the location of, protected property with the intent to shield a military objective from attack, or to shield, favor, or impede military operations, shall be punished as a military commission under this chapter may direct.

(11) TORTURE. —

(A) OFFENSE. — Any person subject to this chapter who commits an act specifically intended to inflict severe physical or mental pain or suffering (other than pain or suffering incidental to lawful sanctions) upon another person within his custody or physical control for the purpose of obtaining information or a confession, punishment, intimidation, coercion, or any reason based on discrimination of any kind, shall be punished, if death results to one or more of the victims, by death or such other punishment as a military commission under this chapter may direct, and, if death does not result to any of the victims, by such punishment, other than death, as a military commission under this chapter may direct.

(B) SEVERE MENTAL PAIN OR SUFFERING DEFINED. — In this paragraph, the term "severe mental pain or suffering" has the meaning given that term in section 2340(2) of title 18.

(12) CRUEL OR INHUMAN TREATMENT. — Any person subject to this chapter who subjects another person in their custody or under their physical control, regardless of nationality or physical location, to cruel or inhuman

treatment that constitutes a grave breach of common Article 3 of the Geneva Conventions shall be punished, if death results to the victim, by death or such other punishment as a military commission under this chapter may direct, and, if death does not result to the victim, by such punishment, other than death, as a military commission under this chapter may direct.

(13) INTENTIONALLY CAUSING SERIOUS BODILY INJURY. —

(A) OFFENSE. — Any person subject to this chapter who intentionally causes serious bodily injury to one or more persons, including privileged belligerents, in violation of the law of war shall be punished, if death results to one or more of the victims, by death or such other punishment as a military commission under this chapter may direct, and, if death does not result to any of the victims, by such punishment, other than death, as a military commission under this chapter may direct.

(B) SERIOUS BODILY INJURY DEFINED. — In this paragraph, the term "serious bodily injury" means bodily injury which involves —

(i) a substantial risk of death;

(ii) extreme physical pain;

(iii) protracted and obvious disfigurement; or

(iv) protracted loss or impairment of the function of a bodily member, organ, or mental faculty.

(14) MUTILATING OR MAIMING. — Any person subject to this chapter who intentionally injures one or more protected persons by disfiguring the person or persons by any mutilation of the person or persons, or by permanently disabling any member, limb, or organ of the body of the person or persons, without any legitimate medical or dental purpose, shall be punished, if death results to one or more of the victims, by death or such other punishment as a military commission under this chapter may direct, and, if death does not result to any of the victims, by such punishment, other than death, as a military commission under this chapter may direct.

(15) MURDER IN VIOLATION OF THE LAW OF WAR. — Any person subject to this chapter who intentionally kills one or more persons, including privileged belligerents, in violation of the law of war shall be punished by death or such other punishment as a military commission under this chapter may direct.

(16) DESTRUCTION OF PROPERTY IN VIOLATION OF THE LAW OF WAR. — Any person subject to this chapter who intentionally destroys property belonging to another person in violation of the law of war shall punished as a military commission under this chapter may direct.

(17) USING TREACHERY OR PERFIDY. — Any person subject to this chapter who, after inviting the confidence or belief of one or more persons that they were entitled to, or obliged to accord, protection under the law of war, intentionally makes use of that confidence or belief in killing, injuring, or capturing such person or persons shall be punished, if death results to one or

more of the victims, by death or such other punishment as a military commission under this chapter may direct, and, if death does not result to any of the victims, by such punishment, other than death, as a military commission under this chapter may direct.

(18) IMPROPERLY USING A FLAG OF TRUCE. — Any person subject to this chapter who uses a flag of truce to feign an intention to negotiate, surrender, or otherwise suspend hostilities when there is no such intention shall be punished as a military commission under this chapter may direct.

(19) IMPROPERLY USING A DISTINCTIVE EMBLEM. — Any person subject to this chapter who intentionally uses a distinctive emblem recognized by the law of war for combatant purposes in a manner prohibited by the law of war shall be punished as a military commission under this chapter may direct.

(20) INTENTIONALLY MISTREATING A DEAD BODY. — Any person subject to this chapter who intentionally mistreats the body of a dead person, without justification by legitimate military necessary, shall be punished as a military commission under this chapter may direct.

(21) RAPE. — Any person subject to this chapter who forcibly or with coercion or threat of force wrongfully invades the body of a person by penetrating, however slightly, the anal or genital opening of the victim with any part of the body of the accused, or with any foreign object, shall be punished as a military commission under this chapter may direct.

(22) SEXUAL ASSAULT OR ABUSE. — Any person subject to this chapter who forcibly or with coercion or threat of force engages in sexual contact with one or more persons, or causes one or more persons to engage in sexual contact, shall be punished as a military commission under this chapter may direct

(23) HIJACKING OR HAZARDING A VESSEL OR AIRCRAFT. — Any person subject to this chapter who intentionally seizes, exercises unauthorized control over, or endangers the safe navigation of a vessel or aircraft that is not a legitimate military objective shall be punished, if death results to one or more of the victims, by death or such other punishment as a military commission under this chapter may direct, and, if death does not result to any of the victims, by such punishment, other than death, as a military commission under this chapter may direct.

(24) TERRORISM. — Any person subject to this chapter who intentionally kills or inflicts great bodily harm on one or more protected persons, or intentionally engages in an act that evinces a wanton disregard for human life, in a manner calculated to influence or affect the conduct of government or civilian population by intimidation or coercion, or to retaliate against government conduct, shall be punished, if death results to one or more of the victims, by death or such other punishment as a military commission under this chapter may direct, and, if death does not result to any of the victims, by such punishment, other than death, as a military commission under this chapter may direct.

(25) PROVIDING MATERIAL SUPPORT FOR TERRORISM. —

(A) OFFENSE. — Any person subject to this chapter who provides material support or resources, knowing or intending that they are to be used in preparation for, or in carrying out, an act of terrorism (as set forth in paragraph (24) of this section), or who intentionally provides material support or resources to an international terrorist organization engaged in hostilities against the United States, knowing that such organization has engaged or engages in terrorism (as so set forth), shall be punished as a military commission under this chapter may direct.

(B) MATERIAL SUPPORT OR RESOURCES DEFINED. — In this paragraph, the term "material support or resources" has the meaning given that term in section 2339A(b) of title 18.

(26) WRONGFULLY AIDING THE ENEMY. — Any person subject to this chapter who, in breach of an allegiance or duty to the United States, knowingly and intentionally aids an enemy of the United States, or one of the co-belligerents of the enemy, shall be punished as a military commission under this chapter may direct.

(27) SPYING. — Any person subject to this chapter who, in violation of the law of war and with intent or reason to believe that it is to be used to the injury of the United States or to the advantage of a foreign power, collects or attempts to collect information by clandestine means or while acting under false pretenses, for the purpose of conveying such information to an enemy of the United States, or one of the co-belligerents of the enemy, shall be punished by death or such other punishment as a military commission under this chapter may direct.

(28) ATTEMPTS. —

(A) IN GENERAL. — Any person subject to this chapter who attempts to commit any offense punishable by this chapter shall be punished as a military commission under this chapter may direct.

(B) SCOPE OF OFFENSE. — An act, done with specific intent to commit an offense under this chapter, amounting to more than mere preparation and tending, even though failing, to effect its commission, is an attempt to commit that offense.

(C) EFFECT OF CONSUMMATION. — Any person subject to this chapter may be convicted of an attempt to commit an offense although it appears on the trial that the offense was consummated.

(29) CONSPIRACY. — Any person subject to this chapter who conspires to commit one or more substantive offenses triable by military commission under this subchapter, and who knowingly does any overt act to effect the object of the conspiracy, shall be punished, if death results to one or more of the victims, by death or such other punishment as a military commission under this chapter may direct, and, if death does not result to any of the victims, by such punishment, other than death, as a military commission under this chapter may direct.

(30) SOLICITATION. — Any person subject to this chapter who solicits or advises another or others to commit one or more substantive offenses triable by military commission under this chapter shall, if the offense solicited or advised is attempted or committed, be punished with the punishment provided for the commission of the offense, but, if the offense solicited or advised is not committed or attempted, shall be punished as a military commission under this chapter may direct.

(31) CONTEMPT. — A military commission under this chapter may punish for contempt any person who uses any menacing word, sign, or gesture in its presence, or who disturbs its proceedings by any riot or disorder.

(32) PERJURY AND OBSTRUCTION OF JUSTICE. — A military commission under this chapter may try offenses and impose such punishment as the military commission may direct for perjury, false testimony, or obstruction of justice related to the military commission.

* * *

SEC. 1807. SENSE OF CONGRESS ON MILITARY COMMISSION SYSTEM.
Pub. L. No. 111–84, § 1807, 123 Stat. 2190, 2614

It is the sense of Congress that — (1) the fairness and effectiveness of the military commissions system under chapter 47A of title 10, United States Code (as amended by section 1802), will depend to a significant degree on the adequacy of defense counsel and associated resources for individuals accused, particularly in the case of capital cases, under such chapter 47A; and (2) defense counsel in military commission cases, particularly in capital cases, under such chapter 47A of title 10, United States Code (as so amended), should be fully resourced as provided in such chapter 47A.

CRIMINAL LAW OF THE PEOPLE'S REPUBLIC OF CHINA

(Adopted at the Second Session of the Fifth National People's Congress on July 1, 1979; revised at the Fifth Session of the Eighth National People's Congress on March 14, 1997 and promulgated by Order No. 83 of the President of the People's Republic of China on March 14, 1997)

Chapter X. Crimes of Servicemen's Transgression of Duties

Article 420. Any act committed by a serviceman in transgression of his duties, an act that endangers the military interests of the State and should therefore be subjected to criminal punishment in accordance with law, constitutes a crime of a serviceman's transgression of duties.

Article 421. Any serviceman who disobeys an order during wartime, thereby jeopardizing a military operation, shall be sentenced to fixed-term imprisonment of not less than three years but not more than 10 years; if heavy losses are caused to a battle or campaign, he shall be sentenced to fixed-term imprisonment of not less than 10 years, life imprisonment, or death.

Article 422. Any serviceman who intentionally conceals or makes a false report about the military situation, refuses to convey a military order or conveys a false military order, thereby jeopardizing a military operation, shall be sentenced to fixed-term imprisonment of not less than three years but not more than 10 years; if heavy losses are caused to a battle or campaign, he shall be sentenced to fixed-term imprisonment of not less than 10 years, life imprisonment, or death.

Article 423. Any serviceman who cares for nothing but saving his skin on the battlefield voluntarily lays down his arms and surrenders to the enemy shall be sentenced to fixed-term imprisonment of not less than three years but not more than 10 years; if the circumstances are serious, he shall be sentenced to fixed-term imprisonment of not less than 10 years or life imprisonment.

Any serviceman who, after surrendering to the enemy, works for the enemy shall be sentenced to fixed-term imprisonment of not less than 10 years, life imprisonment, or death.

Article 424. Any serviceman who deserts from the battlefield shall be sentenced to fixed-term imprisonment of not more than three years; if the circumstances are serious, he shall be sentenced to fixed-term imprisonment of not less than three years but not more than 10 years; if heavy losses are caused to a battle or campaign, he shall be sentenced to fixed-term imprisonment of not less than 10 years, life imprisonment, or death.

Article 425. Any person in command or on duty who leaves his post without permission or neglects his duties, thereby causing serious consequences, shall be sentenced to fixed-term imprisonment of not more than three years or criminal detention; if the consequences are especially serious, he shall be sentenced to fixed-term imprisonment of not less than three years but not more than seven years.

Whoever in wartime commits the crime mentioned in the preceding paragraph shall be sentenced to fixed-term imprisonment of not less than five years.

Article 426. Whoever, by violence or threat, obstructs a commander or a person on duty from performing his duties shall be sentenced to fixed-term imprisonment of not more than five years or criminal detention; if the circumstances are serious, he shall be sentenced to fixed-term imprisonment of not less than five years; if serious injury or death is caused to a person or if there are other especially serious circumstances involved, he shall be sentenced to life imprisonment or death. The punishment for such a crime committed during wartime shall be heavier than in peacetime.

Units which commit the crime of paragraph two of this article are to be sentenced to a fine. The principal leading persons responsible for the crime and other directly responsible personnel are to be punished in accordance with paragraph two of this article.

Article 427. Any officer who abuses his power and instigates his subordinates to act in transgression of their duties, thereby causing serious consequences, shall be sentenced to fixed-term imprisonment of not more than five years or criminal detention; if the circumstances are especially serious, he shall be sentenced to fixed-term imprisonment of not less than five years but not more than 10 years.

Article 428. Any commander who disobeys an order, or flinches before a battle or is inactive in a military operation, thereby causing serious consequences, shall be sentenced to fixed-term imprisonment of not more than five years; if heavy losses are caused during a battle or campaign or if there are other especially serious circumstances involved, he shall be sentenced to fixed-term imprisonment of not less than five years.

Article 429. Any commander on a battlefield who is in a position to rescue the neighborly forces he knows are in a critical situation but does not do so upon request, thus causing heavy losses to the latter, shall be sentenced to fixed-term imprisonment of not more than five years.

Article 430. Any serviceman who, in performing his duties, leaves his post without permission or defects from China or does so when being outside of the country, thus jeopardizing the military interests of the State, shall be sentenced to fixed-term imprisonment of not more than five years or criminal detention; if the circumstances are serious, he shall be sentenced to fixed-term imprisonment of not less than five years.

Any serviceman who, piloting an aircraft or a vessel, defects, or if there are other especially serious circumstances involved, shall be sentenced to fixed-term imprisonment of not less than 10 years, life imprisonment, or death.

Article 431. Whoever, by means of stealing, spying, or buying, illegally obtains military secrets shall be sentenced to fixed-term imprisonment of not more than five years; if the circumstances are serious, he shall be sentenced to fixed-term imprisonment of not less than five years but not more than 10 years; if the circumstances are especially serious, he shall be sentenced to fixed-term imprisonment of not less than 10 years.

Whoever steals, spies into, or buys military secrets for or illegally offers such secrets to agencies, organizations or individuals outside the territory of China shall be sentenced to fixed-term imprisonment of not less than 10 years, life imprisonment, or death.

Article 432. Whoever, in violation of the law and regulations on protection of State secrets, intentionally or negligently divulges military secrets, if the circumstances are serious, shall be sentenced to fixed-term imprisonment of not more than five years or criminal detention; if the circumstances are especially serious, he shall be sentenced to fixed-term imprisonment of not less than five years but not more than 10 years.

Whoever during wartime commits the crime mentioned in the preceding paragraph shall be sentenced to fixed-term imprisonment of not less than five years but not more than 10 years; if the circumstances are especially serious, he shall be sentenced to fixed-term imprisonment of not less than 10 years or life imprisonment.

Article 433. Whoever during wartime fabricates rumors to mislead others and shake the morale of troops shall be sentenced to fixed-term imprisonment of not more than three years; if the circumstances are serious, he shall be sentenced to fixed-term imprisonment of not less than three years but not more than 10 years.

Whoever colludes with the enemy to fabricate rumors so as to mislead others and shake the morale of troops shall be sentenced to fixed-term imprisonment of not less than 10 years or life imprisonment; if the circumstances are especially serious, he may be sentenced to death.

Article 434. Whoever during wartime injures himself in order to evade his military obligation shall be sentenced to fixed-term imprisonment of not more than three years; if the circumstances are serious, he shall be sentenced to fixed-term imprisonment of not less than three years but not more than seven years.

Article 435. Whoever, in violation of the military service law, deserts from the armed forces, if the circumstances are serious, shall be sentenced to fixed-term imprisonment of not more than three years or criminal detention.

Whoever during wartime commits the crime mentioned in the preceding paragraph shall be sentenced to fixed-term imprisonment of not less than three years but not more than seven years.

Article 436. Whoever violates the regulations on the use of weapons and equipment, if the circumstances are serious and an accident leading to serious injury or death of another person occurs due to his neglect of duty, or if there are other serious consequences, shall be sentenced to fixed-term imprisonment of not more than three years or criminal detention; if the consequences are especially serious, he shall be sentenced to fixed-term imprisonment of not less than three years but not more than seven years.

Article 437. Whoever in violation of the regulations on control of weapons and equipment, alters without authorization the use of weapons and equipment allocated, if the consequences are serious, shall be sentenced to fixed-term imprisonment of not more than three years or criminal detention; if the consequences are especially serious, he shall be sentenced to fixed-term imprisonment of not less than three years but not more than seven years.

Article 438. Whoever steals or forcibly seizes weapons, equipment, or military supplies shall be sentenced to fixed-term imprisonment of not more than five years or criminal detention; if the circumstances are serious, he shall be sentenced to fixed-term imprisonment of not less than five years but not more than 10 years; if the circumstances are especially serious, he shall be sentenced to fixed-term imprisonment of not less than 10 years, life imprisonment, or death.

Whoever steals or forcibly seizes firearms, ammunition, or explosives shall be punished in accordance with the provisions of Article 127 of this Law.

Article 439. Whoever illegally sells or transfers weapons or equipment of the armed forces shall be sentenced to fixed-term imprisonment of not less than three years but not more than 10 years; if a large amount of weapons or equipment is sold or transferred or if there are other especially serious circumstances involved, he shall be sentenced to fixed-term imprisonment of not less than 10 years, life imprisonment, or death.

Article 440. Whoever, in violation of an order, abandons weapons or equipment shall be sentenced to fixed-term imprisonment of not more than five years or criminal detention; if he abandons important or a large amount of weapons or equipment or if there are other serious circumstances involved, he shall be sentenced to fixed-term imprisonment of not less than five years.

Article 441. Whoever loses weapons or equipment and fails to report the matter immediately, or if there are other serious circumstances involved, shall be sentenced to fixed-term imprisonment of not more than three years or criminal detention.

Article 442. Where the real estate of the armed forces is sold or transferred in violation of the regulations, if the circumstances are serious, the persons who are directly responsible for the offense shall be sentenced to fixed-term imprisonment of not more than three years or criminal detention; if the circumstances are especially serious, they shall be sentenced to fixed-term imprisonment of not less than three years but not more than 10 years.

Article 443. Any person who abuses his power and maltreats a subordinate, if the circumstances are so flagrant that the victim is seriously injured or if there are other serious consequences, shall be sentenced to fixed-term imprisonment of not more than five years or criminal detention; if he causes death of the victim, he shall be sentenced to fixed-term imprisonment of not less than five years.

Article 444. Where a wounded or sick serviceman is deliberately abandoned on a battlefield, if the circumstances are flagrant, the persons who are directly responsible for the offense shall be sentenced to fixed-term imprisonment of not more than five years.

Article 445. Whoever, being charged with the duty of saving and treating servicemen during wartime, refuses to do so to a serviceman who, though critically sick or wounded, can be saved or treated, shall be sentenced to fixed-term imprisonment of not more than five years or criminal detention; if he causes serious disability or death of the sick or wounded serviceman or if there are other serious circumstances involved, he shall be sentenced to fixed-term imprisonment of not less than five years but not more than 10 years.

Article 446. Any serviceman who, during wartime, cruelly injures innocent residents in an area of military operation or plunders their money or property shall be sentenced to fixed-term imprisonment of not more than five years; if the circumstances are serious, he shall be sentenced to fixed-term imprisonment of not less than five years but not more than 10 years; if the circumstances are especially serious, he shall be sentenced to fixed-term imprisonment of not less than 10 years, life imprisonment, or death.

Article 447. Whoever sets free a prisoner of war without authorization shall be sentenced to fixed-term imprisonment of not more than five years; if he, without authorization, sets free an important prisoner of war or a number of prisoners of war or if there are other serious circumstances involved, he shall be sentenced to fixed-term imprisonment of not less than five years.

Article 448. Whoever maltreats a prisoner of war, if the circumstances are flagrant, shall be sentenced to fixed-term imprisonment of not more than three years.

Article 449. If during wartime a serviceman is sentenced to fixed-term imprisonment of not more than three years for a crime he commits and is granted suspension of sentence because he presents no real danger, he may be allowed to atone for his crime by performing meritorious deeds. If he truly performs meritorious deeds, the original sentence may be rescinded and he shall not be regarded as a criminal.

Article 450. This Chapter shall apply to officers, civilian staff, soldiers in active service and cadets with military status of the Chinese People's Liberation Army, police officers, civilian staff and soldiers in active service and cadets with military status of the Chinese People's Armed Police, and reservists and other persons performing military tasks.

Article 451. The word "wartime" as used in this Law means the time when the State declares the state of war, the armed forces receive tasks of operations, or when the enemy launches a surprise attack.

The time when the armed forces execute martial-law tasks or cope with emergencies of violence shall be regarded as wartime.

DISCIPLINARY REGULATORY ORDER OF THE PEOPLE'S LIBERATION ARMY*
PEOPLE'S REPUBLIC OF CHINA
Central Military Commission, May 4, 2010, effective June 15, 2010

Chapter III. Punishment

Section 1 Purposes and principles of punishment.

Art. 77. The purposes of punishment rest with strict and impartial discipline, educating offending individuals and units, strengthening group unity, and solidifying and raising units' combat ability.

Art. 78. Punishments should adhere to the following principles:

(1) They must be based in facts, and suitably tailored to teach a lesson;

(2) They must adhere to the principle of learning from past errors to avoid future mistakes, and of curing the sickness in order to save the patient;

(3) All individuals must be equal in the face of punishment.

Section 2 Types of Punishment

Art. 79. Punishments for soldiers

(1) Admonition

(2) Stern admonition

(3) A recorded demerit

(4) A recorded significant demerit

(5) Demotion in post or title

(6) Loss of post

(7) Dropping name from the rolls,

(8) Discharge from military service

Of the types of punishment noted in the preceding paragraph, an admonition shall be the least severe form of punishment and discharge from military service shall be the most severe. Demotion of post does not apply to deputy squad leaders. Demotion of title does not apply to privates and corporals/petty officers. For the punishment of demotion of title for sergeants or third class head officers, they shall simultaneously be demoted in officer grade. For demotion in post or demotion in title punishments, typically the offender shall only descend one post or one title. The punishment of dropping name from the roles does not apply to noncommissioned officers.

Art. 80. Types of punishment for commissioned officers and civilian cadres

---

* Translation by John Balzano, Senior Research Scholar in Law, Yale Law School.

(1) Admonition

(2) Stern admonition

(3) A recorded demerit

(4) A recorded significant demerit

(5) Demotion of post (grade) or demotion of title (grade)

(6) Loss of post

(7) Discharge from military service

Of the types of punishment set forth in the preceding paragraph, an admonition shall be the least severe and discharge from military service shall be the most severe. A demotion in post (grade) refers to a demotion in duty grade (specialized technical grade). A demotion in title (grade) refers to a demotion in military officer military title (civilian cadre classification).

Demotion in post (grade) does not apply to platoon grade or specialized technical grade 14 commissioned officers, management personnel and specialized technical grade 14 civilian cadres. A demotion in title (grade) does not apply to second lieutenant officers and grade 9 civilian cadres. For a demotion in post (grade) and a demotion in title (grade), typically there is demotion is only one post (grade) or one title (grade). For commissioned officers and civilian cadres that have lost their posts, they shall at least be treated as one post (grade) less. For platoon grade and specialized technical grade 14 officers and management personnel and specialized technical grade 14 civilian cadres, this treatment of demotion of post (grade) does not apply.

Art. 81. For commissioned officers, civilian cadres, and noncommissioned officers, the same year that they receive a recorded demerit or higher punishment under this order, if they leave work for eight days or more without authorization, if after receiving orders to start work, without proper authorization or a legitimate reason they are late in arriving at their post, their duty wages (specialized technical grade), title wages (in the case of civilian cadre classification), or noncommissioned officer title classification wages, shall, starting in January of the following year, be frozen for one year. Measures for implementing this punishment shall be determined by the general staff department, the general political department, the general logistics department, and the general facilities department.

Section 3 Conditions for Punishment

Art. 82. Upon issuing a public expression, writing or compilation that contains a political misunderstanding; upon publishing a politically problematic article or work; or upon participating in a political organization or a political activity that is prohibited by the military, if the circumstances are less severe, the offender shall receive an admonition or a stern admonition. If the circumstances are more severe, the offender shall receive a recorded demerit or a recorded significant demerit. If the circumstances are very severe, the offender shall receive a demotion in post (grade), a demotion in title (grade) or loss of post.

Art. 83. In the case of inactivity in battle or retreating from the battlefront, if the circumstances are less severe, the offender shall receive a recorded demerit or a recorded significant demerit. If the circumstances are more severe, he shall receive a demotion in post (grade), a demotion in title (grade), or loss of post.

Art. 84. If during combat, a person intentionally harms an innocent resident civilian or intentionally infringes the rights and interests of resident civilians, then, if the circumstances are less severe, the offender shall receive a recorded demerit or a recorded significant demerit, or in more severe circumstances the offender shall receive a demotion in post (grade), a demotion (grade) in title or a loss of post.

Art. 85. In cases of maltreatment of captured personnel, if the circumstances are less severe, the offender shall receive an admonition or a stern admonition. If the circumstances are more severe, the offender shall receive a recorded demerit or a significant recorded demerit. If circumstances are very severe, the offender shall receive a demotion in post (grade), a demotion in title (grade), or a loss of post.

Art. 86. In cases of failing to follow superior orders or commands, whether through the failure to carry out an order or engaging in prohibited conduct, if the circumstances are less severe, the offender shall receive an admonition or a stern admonition. If the circumstances are more severe, the offender shall receive a recorded demerit or a recorded significant demerit. If the circumstances are very severe, the offender shall receive a demotion in post (grade), a demotion in title (grade), or a loss of post.

Art. 87. In cases of a violation of military training requirements, lowering military training quality standards, or influencing the implementation of military training, if the circumstances are less severe the offender shall receive an admonition or a stern admonition. If the circumstances are more severe, the offender shall receive a recorded demerit or a recorded significant demerit, and if the circumstances are very severe, the offender shall receive a demotion in post (grade), a demotion in title (grade), or a loss of post.

Art. 88. In the case of slowness or inactivity that results in an unintentional failure to attend study sessions, work, training, or logistics activities, if the circumstances are less severe, the offender shall receive an admonition or a stern admonition. If the circumstances are more severe, the offender shall receive a recorded demerit or a recorded significant demerit, and if the circumstances are very severe, the offender shall receive a demotion in post (grade), a demotion in title (grade), or a loss of post.

Art. 89. In the case of neglect of duties that causes loss or adverse consequences, if the circumstances are less severe, the offender shall receive an admonition or a stern admonition. If the circumstances are more severe, the offender shall receive a recorded demerit or a significant recorded demerit. If the circumstances are very severe, the offender shall receive a demotion in post (grade), a demotion in title (grade), or a loss of post.

Art. 90. In cases in which fraud or the deception of superiors and the delusion of subordinates or the concealment of information causes negative influence and loss, if the circumstances are less severe, the offender shall receive an admonition or a stern admonition. If the circumstances are more severe, the offender shall receive a recorded demerit or a significant recorded demerit. If the circumstances are very severe, the offender shall receive a demotion in post (grade), a demotion in title (grade), or a loss of post.

Art. 91. In cases where a violation of a regulatory system or of operational rules causes an accident or other loss, if the circumstances are less severe, the offender shall receive an admonition or a stern admonition. If the circumstances are more severe, the offender shall receive a recorded demerit or a significant recorded demerit. If the circumstances are very severe, the offender shall receive a demotion in post (grade), a demotion in title (grade), or a loss of post.

Art. 92. If there is a violation of state or military secret protection regulations, even though it does not cause the leakage or distribution of secret material, it endangers military secret security, if the circumstances are less severe, the offender shall receive an admonition or a stern admonition. If the circumstances are more severe or the case relates to top secret matters, the offender shall receive a recorded demerit or a recorded significant demerit. If the circumstances are very severe, the offender shall receive a demotion in post (grade), a demotion in title (grade), or a loss of post.

If a violation of state or military secret protection regulations causes loss and disclosure, if the circumstances are less severe, the offender shall receive a recorded demerit or a significant recorded demerit; if the circumstances are more severe or the case relates to top secret matters, the offender shall receive a demotion in post (grade) or a demotion in title (grade). If the circumstances are very severe, the offender shall receive a loss of post.

Art. 93. If a person violates regulations by using a mobile phone or by using the international internet, if the circumstances are less severe, the offender shall receive an admonition or a stern admonition. If the circumstances are more severe, the offender shall receive a recorded demerit or a significant recorded demerit. If the circumstances are very severe, the offender shall receive a demotion in post (grade), a demotion in title (grade), or a loss of post.

Art. 94. If a person leaves the country or crosses the border without authorization, if the circumstances are less severe, the offender shall receive a recorded demerit or a significant recorded demerit. If the circumstances are more severe, the offender shall receive a demotion in post (grade), a demotion in title (grade), or a loss of post.

Art. 95. If a person leaves his unit without authorization or unintentionally delays returning to his unit for up to seven days, he shall receive an admonition or stern admonition. If the absence lasts 8 to 15 days, he shall receive a recorded demerit or a significant recorded demerit. If the absence lasts 16 days or longer, he shall receive a demotion in post (grade), a demotion in title (grade), or a loss of post. If the absence is 30 days or over, it shall be dealt with in accordance with Article 119 herein.

Art. 96. If a person gets into a fight or brawl, or participates in a mob or disturbance, if the circumstances are less severe, the offender shall receive an admonition or a stern admonition. If the circumstances are more severe, the offender shall receive a recorded demerit or a significant recorded demerit. If the circumstances are very severe, the offender shall receive a demotion in post (grade), a demotion in title (grade), or a loss of post.

Art. 97. If a person engages in excessive drinking and causes trouble, disturbs the normal order or, after drinking, drives a vehicle or operates weaponry, if the circumstances are less severe, the offender shall receive an admonition or a stern admonition. If the circumstances are more severe, the offender shall receive a recorded demerit or a significant recorded demerit. If the circumstances are very severe, the offender shall receive a demotion in post (grade), a demotion in title (grade), or a loss of post.

Art. 98. If a person gambles, if the circumstances are less severe, the offender shall receive an admonition or a stern admonition. If the circumstances are more severe, the offender shall receive a recorded demerit or a significant recorded demerit. If the circumstances are very severe, the offender shall receive a demotion in post (grade), a demotion in title (grade), or a loss of post.

Art. 99. If a person behaves obscenely toward or subjects a woman to indignities, or if inappropriate sexual behavior occurs, if the circumstances are less severe, the offender shall receive an admonition or a stern admonition. If the circumstances are more severe, the offender shall receive a recorded demerit or a significant recorded demerit. If the circumstances are very severe, the offender shall receive a demotion in post (grade), a demotion in title (grade), or a loss of post.

Art. 100. If a person views or broadcasts obscene materials, if the circumstances are less severe, the offender shall receive an admonition or a stern admonition. If the circumstances are more severe, the offender shall receive a recorded demerit or a significant recorded demerit. If the circumstances are very severe, the offender shall receive a demotion in post (grade), a demotion in title (grade), or a loss of post.

Art. 101. In the case of theft or swindle of public or private property, if the circumstances are less severe, the offender shall receive an admonition or a stern admonition. If the circumstances are more severe, the offender shall receive a recorded demerit or a significant recorded demerit. If the circumstances are very severe, the offender shall receive a demotion in post (grade), a demotion in title (grade), or a loss of post.

Art. 102. In the case of a violation of facility management regulations, and the loss, abandonment, or destruction of facilities, or the unauthorized use, sale, loan or taking of property for himself, if the circumstances are less severe, the offender shall receive an admonition or a stern admonition. If the circumstances are more severe, the offender shall receive a recorded demerit or a significant recorded demerit. If the circumstances are very severe, the offender shall receive a demotion in post (grade), a demotion in title (grade), or a loss of post.

Art. 103. If a person, in violation of regulations, rents, sells or lends military vehicles or license plates or, without authority, sells, copies, rents, lends or gives away military uniforms and their insignia and decorations, if the circumstances are less severe, the offender shall receive an admonition or a stern admonition. If the circumstances are more severe, the offender shall receive a recorded demerit or a significant recorded demerit. If the circumstances are very severe, the offender shall receive a demotion in post (grade), a demotion in title (grade), or a loss of post.

Art. 104. In the case of a violation of administrative regulation on the use of military identification cards and seals, if the circumstances are less severe, the offender shall receive an admonition or a stern admonition. If the circumstances are more severe, the offender shall receive a recorded demerit or a significant recorded demerit. If the circumstances are very severe, the offender shall receive a demotion in post (grade), a demotion in title (grade), or a loss of post.

Art. 105. In the case of a violation of the Provisions on Internal Affairs of the People's Liberation Army regarding military discipline and guidelines on individual conduct, if the circumstances are less severe, the offender shall receive a punishment ranging from an admonition to a significant recorded demerit. If the circumstances are very severe, the offender shall receive a demotion in post (grade) or a demotion in title (grade).

Art. 106. If a person starts a rumor, slanders or frames another individual, if the circumstances are less severe, the offender shall receive an admonition or a stern admonition. If the circumstances are more severe, the offender shall receive a recorded demerit or a significant recorded demerit. If the circumstances are very severe, the offender shall receive a demotion in post (grade), a demotion in title (grade), or a loss of post.

Art. 107. In the case of insult, physical abuse, corporal punishment, or hazing of subordinates, if the circumstances are less severe, the offender shall receive an admonition or a stern admonition. If the circumstances are more severe, the offender shall receive a recorded demerit or a significant recorded demerit. If the circumstances are very severe, the offender shall receive a demotion in post (grade), a demotion in title (grade), or a loss of post.

Art. 108. In cases of abuse of official power, reprisals, or creating difficulties by expressing an individual overly critical opinion or questioning authority and setting forth a complaint against comrades, if the circumstances are less severe, the offender shall receive an admonition or a stern admonition. If the circumstances are more severe, the offender shall receive a recorded demerit or a significant recorded demerit. If the circumstances are very severe, the offender shall receive a demotion in post (grade), a demotion in title grade), or a loss of post.

Art. 109. In cases of failure to rescue a fellow soldier or individual citizens when their lives or property are in danger or when public property is in danger, if the circumstances are less severe, the offender shall receive a stern admonition. If the circumstances are more severe, the offender shall receive a recorded demerit or a significant recorded demerit. If the circumstances are very severe, the offender shall receive a demotion in post (grade), a demotion in title (grade), or a loss of post.

Art. 110. In cases of abuse of power or infringement of the economic rights and interests of soldiers or subordinates or public property, if the circumstances are less severe, the offender shall receive an admonition or a stern admonition. If the circumstances are more severe, the offender shall receive a recorded demerit or a significant recorded demerit. If the circumstances are very severe, the offender shall receive a demotion in post (grade), a demotion in title (grade), or a loss of post.

Art. 111. In cases of corruption and giving and receiving bribes, if the circumstances are less severe, the offender shall receive an admonition or a stern admonition. If the circumstances are more severe, the offender shall receive a recorded demerit or a significant recorded demerit. If the circumstances are very severe, the offender shall receive a demotion in post (grade), a demotion in title (grade), or a loss of post.

Art. 112. In cases of embezzlement, concealment, misappropriation of public funds or property for private use, or other ways of violating financial discipline, if the circumstances are less severe, the offender shall receive an admonition or a stern admonition. If the circumstances are more severe, the offender shall receive a recorded demerit or a significant recorded demerit. If the circumstances are very severe, the offender shall receive a demotion in post (grade), a demotion in title (grade), or a loss of post.

Art. 113. If a person has abused his authority for personal gain in selecting a cadre for a post, choosing a noncommissioned officer, or levying troops, if the circumstances are less severe, the offender shall receive an admonition or a stern admonition. If the circumstances are more severe, the offender shall receive a recorded demerit or a significant recorded demerit. If the circumstances are very severe, the offender shall receive a demotion in post (grade), a demotion in title (grade), or a loss of post.

Art. 114. In cases of participation in business or tax evasion and tax fraud, if the circumstances are less severe, the offender shall receive an admonition or a stern admonition. If the circumstances are more severe, the offender shall receive a recorded demerit or a significant recorded demerit. If the circumstances are very severe, the offender shall receive a demotion in post (grade), a demotion in title (grade), or a loss of post.

Art. 115. In cases of violation of military real estate administrative regulations, unauthorized rental, sale, or transfer of military real estate, unauthorized alteration of military land, or mismanagement of military land that causes it to be depleted, if the circumstances are less severe, the offender shall receive an admonition or a stern admonition. If the circumstances are more severe, the offender shall receive a recorded demerit or a significant recorded demerit. If the circumstances are very severe, the offender shall receive a demotion in post (grade), a demotion in title (grade), or a loss of post.

Art. 116. Exceeding family planning requirements shall result in a demotion in post (grade) or a demotion in title (grade) or greater punishment. In cases of other violations of family planning regulations, if the circumstances are less severe, the offender shall receive an admonition or a stern admonition. If the circumstances are more severe, the offender shall receive a recorded demerit or a significant recorded demerit. If the circumstances are very severe, the offender shall receive a demotion in post (grade), a demotion in title (grade), or a loss of post.

Art. 117. In cases when there is transfer to a different specialty, retirement, or transfer to a different work post (allocation), and there is not an appropriate reason for not reporting according to the stipulated time period (separation from the unit), the offender shall receive an admonition or a stern admonition. If the offender does not comply with the organizational determination and makes trouble unreasonably, and it interferes with the normal order, the offender shall receive a recorded demerit or a significant recorded demerit. If the circumstances are very severe, the offender shall receive a demotion in post (grade), a demotion in title (grade), or a loss of post.

Art. 118. For disciplinary offenses other than those prescribed in articles 82 through 117 of this chapter, the character of the offense, the circumstances, and analogies to similar offenses herein shall determine the punishment, in terms of severity from a stern admonition to a loss of post.

Art. 119. If a conscript violates disciplinary rules and the circumstances are as follows, he shall be dropped from the rolls:

(1) Concealing criminal behavior that occurred before he entered the military or being prosecuted by a local court for criminal responsibility after entering the military;

(2) Without an appropriate reason, repeatedly requesting early retirement from the service and frequently refusing to perform his duties, if after criticism and education the problem is still not corrected;

(3) Unauthorized absence for 30 days or more or overstaying leave for more than 30 days without cause.

Art. 120. If a disciplinary infraction falls into one of the following circumstances, the serviceman shall be discharged from military service:

(1) conduct that constitutes a crime of endangering state security;

(2) committing an intentional crime for which the sentence is over five years of incarceration, life imprisonment, or the death penalty;

(3) being sentenced to less than five years for a crime or being sentenced to more than five years for a negligent crime while serving time, or being sentenced to re-education through labor while serving time for that, and refusal to reform under grave circumstances;

(4) violation of disciplinary rules under severe circumstances, with an abominable influence, and there has already been a loss of basic military qualifications.

Art. 121. Personnel who have violated criminal law and have been duly prosecuted according to law, but who do not fulfill the conditions in Article 120 for discharge from military service, shall receive a demotion in post (grade), a demotion in title (grade), a loss of post, or the dropping from the rolls as punishment.

Section Four Limits of Authority Concerning Punishment

Art. 122. The limits on imposing punishments on servicemen shall be as follows:

(1) An admonition shall be ratified by the company;

(2) A stern admonition shall be ratified by the battalion;

(3) A recorded demerit, significant recorded demerit, demotion in post and loss of post shall be ratified by the regiment or the brigade;

(4) Dropping from the rolls and discharge from military service must be ratified by army command.

The limits on punishment of noncommissioned officers shall be as follows:

(1) For initial and middle grade noncommissioned officers, admonitions shall be approved by the company, stern admonitions by the battalion, recorded demerits and recorded significant demerits, demotion of grade, and loss of post shall be approved by the regiment or brigade, and discharges from military service shall be approved by army command.

(2) For senior noncommissioned officers, admonitions shall be approved by the battalion commander, stern admonitions by the regiment or the brigade commander, recorded demerits or recorded significant demerits shall be approved by the brigade or the division, and discharges from military service shall be ratified by the regional army command.

The punishment of demotion of title for privates shall be implemented according to limits on authority prescribed in the Law on Compulsory Military Service regarding the ratification of the bestowal and promotion of title.

Art. 123. The limits on punishment of commissioned officers and civilian cadres shall be as follows:

(1) Platoon grade or specialized technical grade 14 commissioned officers and for officer work grade and specialized technical grade 14 civilian cadres admonitions and stern admonitions shall be ratified by the battalion, recorded demerits and recorded significant demerits shall be ratified by the regiment or the brigade and discharge from military service shall be ratified by the regional army command.

(2) For company grade and specialized technical grades 13 and 12 commissioned officers and science personnel grade and specialized technical grades 13 and 12 civilian cadres, admonitions and stern admonitions, recorded demerits and recorded significant demerits shall be ratified by the regiment or brigade and discharge from military service shall be ratified by the regional army command.

(3) For battalion grade and specialized technical grades 11 and 10 commissioned officers and science grade and specialized technical grades 11 and 10 civilian cadres, admonitions and stern admonitions shall be ratified by the regiment or the brigade and recorded demerits and recorded significant demerits shall be ratified by the brigade commander or the division commander and discharge from military service shall be ratified by the regional army command.

(4) For regiment grade and specialized technical grades 9, 8, and 7 (middle grade specialized technical services) commissioned officers and section grade and specialized technical grades 9, 8, and 7 (middle grade specialized technical services) civilian cadres, admonitions and stern admonitions shall be ratified by the division, recorded demerits and recorded significant demerits shall be ratified by army command, and discharge from military service shall be ratified by the regional army command. For deputy-regimental commander posts and specialized technical grade 9 commissioned officers, and deputy section and specialized technical grade 9 civilian cadres, the brigade may ratify admonitions and stern admonitions.

(5) For division grade and specialized technical grades 7 (high grade specialized technical services), 6, 5, and 4 commissioned officers, and bureau grade and specialized technical grades 7 (high grade specialized technical services), 6, 5, and 4 civilian cadres, admonitions and stern admonitions shall be ratified by an army commander, recorded demerits

and recorded significant demerits shall be ratified by the regional army command, and discharge from military service shall be ratified by the Central Military Commission.

(6) General grade and specialized technical grade three and higher commissioned officers and civilian cadres admonitions and stern admonitions shall be ratified by the regional army command and recorded demerits and recorded significant demerits and discharge from military service shall be ratified by the Central Military Commission. For recorded demerits and recorded significant demerit punishments, the Central Military Commission may delegate to the General Political Department the power to examine and approve these types of punishment.

(7) For regional army command officers, the Central Military Commission shall ratify punishments.

Demotion of post (grade) and loss of post punishments shall be effected in accordance with the provisions on the limits of appointment and removal of commissioned officers in the Military Officer Law and the regulations of the Central Military Commission. Demotion of title shall be effected in accordance with the PLA Regulations on Military Commissioned Officers' Titles. Demotion of post for civilian cadres shall be effected in accordance with the rules of the General Political Department.

Military regions, other similarly ranked entities, and Party committees at the army command level can entrust that grade's political organs to examine and ratify punishments of recorded demerit and recorded significant demerit.

When entities at the regiment level and above examine and ratify punishments of admonition, stern admonition, recorded demerit, and recorded significant demerit, they shall report to the Party committee with the administrative appointment and removal power over the punished commissioned officers or civilian cadres (specialized technical grade) for recordation and filing.

When a high grade specialized technical commissioned officer or civilian cadre receive punishments of a demotion in post (grade), a demotion in title (grade) or discharge from post, that shall be reported to the General Political Department for recordation and filing.

Art. 124. The various headquarters departments, various branches of the armed forces, military universities of military science, and National Defense University shall have punishment powers within their military region.

Art. 125. The naval fleet, air force, and other similar units may ratify the punishment of discharge from military service for deputy regimental commanders and specialized technical grade 9 and below commissioned officers and deputy section grade and specialized technical grade 9 and below civilian cadres; they may ratify the punishments of recorded demerit and recorded significant demerit for division grade and specialized technical grades 7 (high grade specialized technical services), 6, 5, and 4 commissioned officers and bureau grade and specialized technical grades 7 (high grade specialized technical services), 6, 5, and 4 civilian cadres; and they may ratify the punishments of admonition and stern admonition for lieutenant generals and specialized technical grade 3 commissioned officers and specialized technical grade three civilian cadres.

Art. 126. Company, battalion, regiment, division, and general grade units shall have punishment powers within those respective entities.

Art. 127. Various levels of the headquarters department, the political department (section), the logistics department (section), the facilities department (section) and other related levels of organs shall have jurisdiction for punishment of subordinate units (parts) directly under their supervision or personnel that belong to their departments.

Art. 128. Personnel who have left their original unit and have been temporarily detailed by their command to attend a training assembly and execute immediate tasks shall be subject to punishment in accordance with these provisions by the receiving command from their current unit (with advice from their permanent unit) if they commit a disciplinary offense.

The established Party committee within the current unit may, according to the clear jurisdiction of the superior grade, impose punishment on the individual who has committed the disciplinary offense.

Art. 129. Middle school graduates and privates recruited into cadet school shall be punished according to limits set for the punishment of privates. Punishment of those who have already enlisted but have not yet assumed their posts, graduated from the national defense university in a specialized technical grade, directly entered military work after graduating from an institution of higher learning, military graduate students that were enrolled in and graduated from typical higher learning school, and military school graduates that have still not assumed their post or specialized technical grade shall be in accordance with the limits for punishment of platoon and specialized technical grade 4 commissioned officers. Commissioned officers and civilian cadres who are in school shall be subject to punishment according to the limits prescribed for their current post or specialized technical grade.

Art. 130. Commissioned officers and civilian cadres who already have an administrative post and a specialized technical grade shall be subject to punishment according to the limits prescribed for the higher administrative post or specialized technical grade.

Art. 131. Punishments shall ordinarily be imposed in accordance with these limits on authority set forth herein. If required by personnel allocations or special circumstances, a superior can override the grade distinction and impose a punishment on a subordinate.

Section Five Imposition of Punishments

Art. 132. Punishment shall be imposed on the basis of the facts and circumstances of the offense, its character, and its influence and the accused's contrition. Punishment shall be carefully imposed in accordance with the categories of punishment, criteria, and procedures prescribed in these regulations.

Two or more types of disciplinary infractions committed at the same time shall be dealt with together and the punishment shall be increased.

For one instance of a type of disciplinary infraction or multiple types, there can be only one imposition of punishment.

Art. 133. Punishment may be reduced or mitigated under the following circumstances:

(1) The offender admits his guilt or returns the benefits of the violation of law or disciplinary rules;

(2) The offender informs the authorities of the wrong of co-actors, and an investigation proves that his account is true;

(3) The offender retracts the loss and influence or actively thwarts a harmful result from occurring or developing.

Art. 134. Punishment may be increased or made more onerous under the following circumstances:

(1) The problem is concealed or the individual refuses to admit his guilty and fabricates, destroys, or hides evidence;

(2) When two or more persons jointly violate disciplinary rules, anyone who plays a primary role in the offense;

(3) A person violates disciplinary rules and forces or entices others to violate disciplinary rules as well;

(4) Covering up of the joint violations of others or thwarting others from reporting those violations, acknowledging the wrong, or providing evidence;

(5) Other behavior that interferes with or obstructs the investigation and punishment of disciplinary violations.

Art. 135. Punishment shall be imposed in accordance with the following procedures:

(1) The senior cadre's organization or managing organ shall take responsibility for investigating and confirming the facts underlying a disciplinary offense and it shall produce written materials;

(2) The Party committee (branch) shall convene a meeting to examine and determine the punishment for an offender. If the offense falls outside of the limits of that grade's authority, it shall be reported to the next higher grade's Party committee for examination and determination;

(3) According to the Party committee's (branch) determination, the senior officer of the ratifying entity shall impose punishment.

In extraordinary circumstances, the senior officer can directly determine the punishment for a member of his unit but he must thereafter report the action taken to the Party committee (branch) and take responsibility for the decision.

Art. 136. Swift resolution should be sought against the offender. An offense should ordinarily be punished within 45 days of discovery. If this period needs to be extended due to complex facts or special circumstances, the next higher grade must grant approval.

Art. 137. Before the decision on punishment is announced, the person who is to receive punishment shall be heard in person. If the person is dissatisfied with the result, he may appeal within 10 days of receipt of the decision. The punishment may not be executed during the appeal period.

Art. 138. The punishment decision shall be transmitted in either oral or written form. It shall be announced before the troops or during a meeting and it may be circulated in writing or announced only to the person being punished. Written transmittal of punishment decisions shall be issued in a general order style. Written and oral transmittal of punishment decisions must include a "Punishment Register (report) Form" (an example is attached as appendix 4) [omitted here]. After the punishment has been announced, the Punishment Register (report) form, the punishment general order and other relevant materials shall be put into the person's service record.

Art. 139. Six months after a person receives an admonition or a stern admonition, 12 months after a person receives a recorded demerit or a recorded significant demerit, 18 months after a person receives a demotion in post (grade), a demotion in title (grade), and 24 months after a person receives a loss of post, if the person has truly corrected the wrong, the punishment may no longer affect promotions for posts or titles (grades). If there is a special contribution, a person who receives punishment may not be subject to the time limits above.

Art. 140. A soldier who meets the criteria for dropping from the rolls and reeducation through labor shall first undergo reeducation through labor and only thereafter be dropped from the rolls.

Art. 141. When commissioned officers and civilian cadres who have both an administrative post and a specialized technical grade receive a punishment of demotion in post (grade), then according to the character of the violation, the circumstances, and the result, either their administrative post or their specialized technical grade shall be downgraded. If the political or living conditions do not change, then they shall be downgraded by the higher of the administrative post or the specialized technical grade.

Art. 142. When commissioned officers and civilian cadres who have both an administrative post and a specialized technical grade receive a punishment of loss of post, then according the character, the circumstances, and the result, they may lose both their administrative post and their specialized technical post, or they may lose only their administrative post. If the disciplinary infraction relates to the level of specialized technical grade or if the circumstances are such that it is not appropriate for them to continue to hold the specialized technical position then they shall lose their administrative post and specialized technical grade simultaneously.

When commissioned officers and civilian cadres who have both an administrative post and a specialized technical grade receive a punishment of loss of post, then their political and living conditions shall be defined as follows:

(1) If the administrative post is at or above the level of the specialized technical grade, then the demotion in administrative post shall have priority. If the newly defined administrative post's grade is below the original specialized technical grade, the specialized technical grade shall be reduced to a corresponding grade.

(2) If the grade of the administrative post is lower than that of the specialized technical grade, demotion in specialized technical grade shall have priority. If the new defined specialized technical grade is below that of the original administrative post grade, the administrative post grade shall be reduced correspondingly.

Art. 143. When a serviceman receives a punishment of being dropped from the rolls, the battalion level command shall issue a written punishment proposal, the regiment and brigade commands shall investigate the essential facts, and after the brigade and division commanders review this, they shall report to the army level command for ratification.

Art. 144. Soldiers dropped from the rolls shall have their title and original post automatically cancelled. They shall not receive state retirement benefits for soldiers. When they leave the unit, they shall not go through retirement procedures. The approving authority shall issue a certificate and a designated individual shall send the service record to the original conscripting county (administrative district) People's Military Department.

The county level (administrative district) People's Military Department of personnel who have been dropped from the rolls shall immediately receive them and assist in managing their settlement in the area. The service record entries shall go through relevant procedures and will be circulated within the county (administrative district).

Art. 145. Soldiers who have been discharged from military service shall have their military title cancelled and any awards received during their period of service, original posts, and grades shall be automatically cancelled. They shall not receive state retirement benefits for soldiers. When they leave their unit, they shall not go through retirement procedures. Instead, the approving authority shall issue a certificate and shall designate the person for return to society.

The county level military department shall report the discharge within the county.

UNITED NATIONS TRANSITIONAL ADMINISTRATION IN EAST TIMOR
CODE OF MILITARY DISCIPLINE FOR THE DEFENCE FORCE OF EAST TIMOR
Regulation No. 2001/12 (2001)

Section 1.   Definitions

Wherever used in the present Regulation, the following terms shall have the following meanings:

(a)   "accused" means the member of the Defence Force subject to this Code of Military Discipline in respect of whom disciplinary proceedings are conducted into an alleged breach of service discipline.

(b)   "breach of service discipline" means each of the acts or omissions described in Section 4 of the present Regulation, including the elements of each as provided in the annex attached hereto.

(c)   "charge" means a formal accusation in the prescribed form, prepared at the direction of the disciplinary officer, that a member of the Defence Force subject to this Code of Military Discipline has committed a breach of service discipline.

(d)   "Chief of the Defence Force" means the Chief of the Defence Force of East Timor as appointed by the Transitional Administrator pursuant to Section 4.2 of UNTAET Regulation No. 2001/1.

(e)   "Code of Military Discipline" means this Code of Military Discipline for the Defence Force of East Timor as established in Section 2 of the present Regulation.

(f)   "Defence Force" means the Defence Force of East Timor as established pursuant to UNTAET Regulation No. 2001/1, and includes both the Regular and Reserve components.

(g)   "disciplinary officer" means:

   (i)   the Chief of the Defence Force; or

   (ii) an officer not below the rank of Major appointed in writing by the Chief of the Defence Force to be a disciplinary officer for such period and with such provisos as the Chief of the Defence Force deems proper.

(h)   "disciplinary proceedings" means the investigation into, hearing of and decision, under the present Regulation, on a allegation of a breach of service discipline and includes a review of any such decision.

(i)   "investigating officer" means an officer, Chief Sergeant or Sergeant Major of the Defence Force tasked with the investigation of an alleged breach of service discipline pursuant to Section 6 of the present Regulation.

(j)   "member of the Defence Force" means an officer or enlisted rank in either the Regular or Reserve component of the Defence Force.

Section 2.   Code of Military Discipline

The Code of Military Discipline for the Defence Force of East Timor is hereby established.

Section 3.   Application

3.1 All members of the Regular component of the Defence Force are subject to this Code of Military Discipline at all times.

3.2 Members of the Reserve component of the Defence Force are subject to this Code of Military Discipline whilst on duty.

Section 4.   Breaches of Service Discipline

Any member of the Defence Force subject to this Code of Military Discipline who commits any of the following shall commit a breach of service discipline and shall be liable on conviction to any punishment laid down in Section 9 of the present Regulation:

(a)   the ill-treatment in any way of a member of the Defence Force of inferior rank or a subordinate;

(b)   the offering, in the course of duty, of inhumane or degrading treatment to another member of the Defence Force;

(c)   the causing or engaging in a disturbance or behavior in a disorderly manner;

(d)   behavior in an insubordinate manner;

(e)   whilst on watch or sentry duty either

   (i)   the engaging in misconduct, or

   (ii) the failure to do one's duty;

(f)   disobedience of a lawful order;

(g)   disobedience of a lawful general order;

(h)   drunkenness if, owing to the influence of alcohol or any drug, whether alone or in combination with any other circumstances:

     (i)   unfitness to be entrusted with his duty,

     (ii)   unfitness to be entrusted with any duty which he was reasonably aware that he could be called upon to perform,

     (iii)   behavior in a disorderly manner, or

     (iv)   behavior in any manner likely to bring discredit on the Defence Force;

(i)   absence without leave;

(j)   avoidance of duty;

(k)   the making of a false statement concerning any official matter relating to the Defence Force;

(l)   without reasonable excuse, fighting with another member of the Defence Force;

(m)   the willful or by willful neglect damaging or causing damage to or the loss of any property of the Defence Force;

(n)   conduct prejudicial to good order or military discipline or behavior in a manner which brings discredit on the Defence Force.

Section 5.   Arrest

5.1 Any member of the Defence Force subject to this Code of Military Discipline found committing a breach of service discipline, or reasonably suspected of committing or having committed a breach of service discipline, may be arrested in accordance with the provisions of this Section.

5.2 A member of the Defence Force subject to this Code of Military Discipline may be arrested by a member of the Defence Force of superior rank.

5.3 As soon as possible, but in any event no later than 24 hours following arrest, the arrested member of the Defence Force must be informed of the reasons for his arrest.

5.4 Within 24 hours of arrest, a disciplinary officer must be informed and must consider the necessity of retaining the member of the Defence Force in arrest, and the disciplinary officer shall order the release of the arrested member of the Defence Force unless he reasonably believes that if released:

     (a)   the arrested member of the Defence Force will absent himself or flee disciplinary proceedings;

     (b)   there is a risk that evidence will be lost, tainted or destroyed; or

     (c)   the arrested member of the Defence Force will commit further breaches of service discipline if released.

5.5 If, in accordance with Section 5.4 of the present Regulation, the disciplinary officer shall have determined the member of the Defence Force under arrest shall be further retained, the period of such further retention shall not exceed 24 hours, and the disciplinary officer must notify the local prosecutor of the arrest.

5.6 Before the expiry of the period of 48 hours of arrest, the disciplinary officer must have either released the member of the Defence Force under arrest from arrest under this Section or dealt with the allegation of the breach of service discipline upon which the arrest is based.

Section 6.   Investigation of Breaches of Service Discipline

6.1 An allegation that a member of the Defence Force subject to this Code of Military Discipline has committed a breach of discipline shall be reported to a disciplinary officer, who shall investigate each such allegation and, in doing so, may task an investigating officer.

6.2 One or more investigating officers may investigate a breach of service discipline, which investigation shall be conducted in accordance with procedures for investigations of breaches of service discipline to be prescribed by the Chief of the Defence Force in subsequent administrative instructions.

6.3 If, as a result of an investigation conducted in accordance with this Section 6, the disciplinary officer determines to charge a member of the Defence Force with a breach of service discipline, charges shall be preferred in accordance with procedures for charging a member of the Defence Force with a breach of service discipline to be prescribed by the Chief of the Defence Force in subsequent administrative instructions.

Section 7.   Jurisdiction of Disciplinary Officers

7.1 The Chief of the Defence Force:

    (a)   has jurisdiction over all breaches of service discipline; and

    (b)   may impose any punishment provided in Section 9.1 of the present Regulation for such breach of service discipline.

7.2 A disciplinary officer:

    (a)   has jurisdiction over all breaches of service discipline by accused junior in rank to the disciplinary officer; and

    (b)   may impose any punishment provided in Section 9.1 of the present Regulation for such a breach of service discipline.

Section 8.   Procedures at Disciplinary Hearings

8.1 Disciplinary proceedings are not judicial proceedings.

8.2 An accused shall be considered as innocent until proven guilty.

8.3 Disciplinary officers shall not be bound by technical rules of law or evidence and may inform themselves on any matter relevant to the alleged breach of service discipline as the disciplinary officer considers reasonably necessary for the purposes of the disciplinary hearing; provided, however,

    (a)   the disciplinary hearing shall at all times be conducted in a manner that is fair and just; and

(b) all evidence presented at a disciplinary hearing shall be given on oath or affirmation.

8.4 Disciplinary hearings shall be conducted in a manner that provides to the accused a full and fair opportunity to present a defence or explanation, and for that purpose and to that extent an accused is entitled:

(a) to have the charge reduced into writing;

(b) to have a copy of the charge before the disciplinary hearing commences;

(c) to have the charge explained before the commencement of the disciplinary hearing by a superior officer or at the disciplinary hearing by the disciplinary officer;

(d) to question witnesses called against the accused and persons whose statements are used against the accused;

(e) to call and question witnesses on the accused's behalf;

(f) to give evidence in his own defence, to provide an explanation of his actions and of mitigating factors and to have such evidence or explanation recorded in writing; and

(g) to be represented by a member of the Defence Force of the accused's own choosing, provided that member is reasonably available and not connected with the investigation or conduct of the disciplinary proceedings.

8.5 A disciplinary officer may conclude that an accused is guilty of the breach of service discipline for which the accused has been subjected to a disciplinary hearing only if the disciplinary officer, considering all of the evidence available, is sure that each of the elements of the breach of service discipline as set forth in the annex attached hereto has been established.

8.6 The findings of the disciplinary officer in relation to each disciplinary hearing, and any punishment awarded in connection therewith, including determinations relating to defences, explanations and mitigating factors, shall be recorded in writing.

8.7 If, at any stage of the disciplinary proceedings, before any punishment has been imposed, the disciplinary officer, of his own motion or at the request of the accused, determines that in the interests of justice he should not deal with the charge, then he may transfer the matter to another disciplinary officer.

Section 9. Punishments for Breaches of Service Discipline

9.1 The disciplinary officer, taking into account such factors as may be relevant in determining the same, may impose the following punishments, listed in descending order of severity, on a member of the Defence Force found guilty of committing a breach of service discipline:

(a) detention for a period not exceeding 7 days;

(b) confinement to barracks for a period not exceeding 7 days;

(c)   a fine not exceeding the equivalent of 2 days' pay;

(d)   stoppage of leave for a period not exceeding 7 days;

(e)   extra duties for a period not exceeding 7 days; or

(f)   reprimand,

provided, however, that at any disciplinary hearing addressing more than one breach of service discipline,

(g)   the total period of detention may not exceed 28 days;

(h)   the total period of confinement to barracks may not exceed 28 days;

(i)   the total fine imposed may not exceed the equivalent of 8 days' pay;

(j)   the total stoppage of leave imposed may not exceed 28 days; and

(k)   the total number of extra duties imposed may not exceed 28 days;

and, provided further, that detention may only be imposed for a member below the rank of Sargento Ajudante.

9.2 The Chief of the Defence Force may, by subsequent administrative instruction, make rules in relation to punishments for breaches of service discipline.

Section 10.   Review of Decisions in Disciplinary Proceedings

10.1 The Chief of the Defence Force may, of his own motion or at the request of any member of the Defence Force affected by the decision emanating from a disciplinary hearing, review such decision and, if he deems proper in the interests of justice to do so, may:

(a)   disallow any finding of guilt; or

(b)   impose any punishment less than that imposed by the decision

and, for the purposes of a review, may suspend the carrying out, or the continuance, of any punishment imposed.

10.2 The Transitional Administrator or his civilian delegate may, of his own motion or at the request of any member of the Defence Force affected by the decision emanating from a disciplinary hearing, review a decision of the Chief of the Defence Force in connection with such disciplinary proceedings and, if he deems proper in the interests of justice to do so, may:

(a)   disallow any finding of guilt; or

(b)   impose any punishment less than that imposed by the decision

and, for the purposes of a review, may suspend the carrying out, or the continuance, of any punishment imposed.

10.3 When a member of the Defence Force affected by a decision emanating from a disciplinary hearing requests a review under Sections 10.1 or 10.2 of the present Regulation,

(a)   the request must be made in writing within 30 days of the completion of the disciplinary hearing, and

(b)   further proceedings in connection with such disciplinary proceedings shall be stayed until such time as the requesting the review shall have been completed.

Section 11.   Administrative Instructions

11.1 The Transitional Administrator may issue administrative instructions and other instruments prescribing all matters that are necessary or convenient to be prescribed in connection with the implementation of the present Regulation.

11.2 The Chief of the Defence Force may issue administrative instructions, not inconsistent with this Regulation, on matters relating but not limited to:

(a)   the appointment of members of the Defence Force as disciplinary officers to exercise disciplinary powers as set out in this Regulation;

(b)   the rank of members of the Defence Force that a disciplinary officer may exercise disciplinary power over in accordance with this Code of Military Discipline;

(c)   the procedures to be followed in the investigation of breaches of service discipline;

(d)   the procedure for charging an accused with a breach of service discipline;

(e)   the procedure for a disciplinary hearing into a breach of service discipline;

(f)   the number and combination of punishments that may be imposed by a disciplinary officer; and

(g)   the consequences of any punishment listed in Section 9 of the present Regulation.

Section 12.   Reference of Matter to Civil Authorities

12.1 If, in the course of any disciplinary proceedings, the disciplinary officer shall form the opinion that a member of the Defence Force may have committed a civil criminal offence, the disciplinary officer shall as soon as practicable advise the appropriate civil law enforcement or judiciary authorities of that opinion and the reasons for it.

12.2 If, following notification to civil authorities pursuant to Section 12.1 of the present Regulation, the disciplinary proceedings should conclude prior to the conclusion of the civilian criminal justice process with respect to the alleged civil criminal offence, no decision of the disciplinary proceedings shall in any way constitute a defence or other impediment to such civilian criminal justice proceedings.

Section 13.   Entry into Force

The present Regulation shall enter into force upon signature.

[Elements of the breaches of service discipline set out in § 4 were prescribed in an Annex.]

FEDERAL CONSTITUTIONAL LAW ON COURTS-MARTIAL OF THE RUSSIAN FEDERATION
No. 1-ФКЗ, June 23, 1999*

CHAPTER III STATUS OF COURTS-MARTIAL JUDGES

* A. Arbatov & E. Chernikov (eds.), Russian Federation Legal Acts on Civil-Military Relations. Collection of Documents, Moscow 2003, 675 pp. ISBN 5-93111-027-5.

CHAPTER I.   GENERAL PROVISIONS

Article 1.   Courts-Martial of the Russian Federation

1. Courts-martial of the Russian Federation (hereinafter referred to as courts-martial) shall form a part of the Court System of the Russian Federation, be federal courts of common jurisdiction and execute judicial power in the Armed Forces of the Russian Federation, other troops, military formations and federal bodies of executive power (hereinafter referred to as bodies) in which military service is envisaged according to federal law.

2. Courts-martial shall be formed on the principle of territory in the place of stationing of military units and institutions of the Armed Forces of the Russian Federation, other troops, military formations and bodies. Courts-martial shall be situated in places open for free access.

3. Courts-martial shall be organized and cancelled in accordance with federal law. No court-martial may be cancelled if the matters that were submitted to it were not immediately transferred to the jurisdiction of another court. The number of courts-martial and the number of judges of courts-martial shall be determined by the Supreme Court of the Russian Federation.

4. During times of mobilization and in wartime the peculiarities of organization and functioning of courts-martial shall be defined by relevant Federal Constitutional Laws.

Article 2.   Legislation of the Russian Federation on Courts-Martial

The powers, the order of organization and functioning of courts-martial shall be determined by the Constitution of the Russian Federation, Federal Constitutional Law on Judicial System of the Russian Federation, this Federal Constitutional Law, other Federal Constitutional laws, and federal laws.

Article 3.   Courts-Martial Administer Justice

Courts-martial administer justice on behalf of the Russian Federation, considering cases in civil, administrative and criminal legal proceedings.

Article 4.   Main Tasks of Courts-Martial

While considering cases, the main tasks of courts-martial shall be provision and protection:

of infringed and/or questioned rights, freedoms and interests of an individual and citizen, entities and their formations that are protected by law;

of infringed and/or questioned rights and interests of local self government that are protected by law;

of infringed and/or questioned rights and protected by law interests of the Russian Federation, bodies of the Russian Federation, federal agencies of State power, and agencies of State power of the bodies of the Russian Federation.

Article 5.   Independence of Courts-Martial and Independence of Judges of Courts-Martial

1. Courts-martial shall administer justice independently, and are subordinate only to the Constitution of the Russian Federation, Federal Constitutional Laws and federal laws.

2. Judges of courts-martial shall be independent and in their activities of administering justice they shall not report to anyone.

3. Any interference in the activities of the judges of courts-martial concerning administering justice shall be impermissible and shall lead to responsibility under federal law.

4. The guarantees of judges' independence determined by the Constitution of the Russian Federation, Federal Constitutional Laws and federal laws, shall not be cancelled or reduced in respect to the judges of courts-martial.

Article 6.   Language of Legal Proceedings and Records in Courts-Martial

Legal proceedings and records in courts-martial shall be conducted in the state language of the Russian Federation — in the Russian language. The individuals who participate in the proceedings and who do not know the Russian language shall be given the right to speak and to give evidence in their native language or in any other language that they choose voluntarily, and to use an interpreter's services.

Article 7. Cases within the Competence of Courts-Martial

1. The following cases shall be within the competence of courts-martial:

(1) civil and administrative cases about infringed and/or questioned rights, freedoms and protected by law interests of military persons of the Armed Forces of the Russian Federation, other troops, military formations and bodies (hereinafter referred to as military personnel), citizens who are attending military periodical training, from actions (inaction) of authorities of Military Office, military officials and from the decisions taken by them;

(2) cases about crimes with which the following individuals are charged: military persons, citizens who are attending military periodical training and citizens who are discharged from military service and citizens who have passed military periodical training — on the condition that these crimes were committed by them during the time of military service or military periodical training;

(3) cases about administrative offenses that were committed by military persons and citizens who are attending military periodical training.

2. Citizens who were discharged from military service and citizens who have passed military periodical training shall have the right to appeal to a court-martial against actions (or inaction) of authorities of Military Office, military officials and against decisions taken by them that infringe the rights, freedoms and protected by law interests of the above mentioned citizens during their military service and military periodical training.

3. The jurisdiction of cases about administrative offenses and cases about crimes with which the following individuals are charged: military persons, citizens who are attending military periodical training and citizens who are discharged from military service and citizens who have passed military periodical training who have committed offenses during the time of military service or military periodical training and the civil — shall be determined by corresponding federal procedure laws.

4. Courts-martial which are located outside the territory of the Russian Federation shall have jurisdiction over all civil, administrative and criminal cases that are to be submitted to federal courts of common jurisdiction if it is not determined otherwise under the International Treaty of the Russian Federation.

5. Courts-martial shall not have jurisdiction over cases about crimes of which military persons and citizens who are attending military periodical training, are accused on the condition that these crimes have been committed by them before enrollment into military service or military periodical training.

6. Courts-martial examine appeals against the application by an official who is making an inquiry, by an investigator or prosecutor the measure of taking into custody and prolongation by the above mentioned officials the period of taking into custody military persons and citizens who are attending military periodical trainings and also claims against actions (or inaction) of military prosecutors and decisions adopted by them in respect to military persons and citizens who are attending military periodical training.

7. Within their competence and in the order determined by federal law, courts-martial shall consider cases and materials connected with the limitations

of constitutional freedoms and rights to confidentiality of correspondence, telephone and any other conversations, post, telegraph and other messages, and inviolability of home.

8. The jurisdiction of courts-martial and the order of administering of justice during times of mobilization and in wartime shall be determined by corresponding Federal Constitutional Laws.

CHAPTER II.   SYSTEM AND POWERS OF COURTS-MARTIAL

Article 8.   System of Courts-Martial

1. The following courts constitute the systems of courts-martial: district (fleet) courts martial and garrison courts-martial.

2. When a military unit, enterprise, institution or organization of the Armed Forces of the Russian Federation, other troops, military formations and bodies are located outside the territory of the Russian Federation, courts martial may be formed in the place of their dislocation if it is envisaged according to an International Treaty of the Russian Federation.

Article 9.   Powers of the Supreme Court of the Russian Federation to Examine Cases within the Jurisdiction of Courts-Martial

1. The Presidium of the Supreme Court of the Russian Federation shall consider cases concerning appeals against decisions, convictions, definitions and judgments of the Military Chamber of the Supreme Court of the Russian Federation (hereinafter referred to as the Military Chamber) and of courts-martial upon these documents have entered into force.

2. The Cassation Chamber of the Supreme Court of the Russian Federation shall consider cases concerning complaints and appeals against decisions, convictions, definitions and judgments of the Military Chamber that were adopted in the first instance by it and have not entered into force yet.

3. The Military Chamber shall consider in the first instance:

(1) cases concerning appeals against non-regulatory acts issued by the President of the Russian Federation, regulation acts issued by the Government of the Russian Federation, the Defense Ministry of the Russian Federation, other federal bodies of executive power in which military service is envisaged under federal law, and related to rights, freedoms and protected by law interests of military persons and citizens who have periodical military training;

(2) cases concerning crimes of which a judge of a military court is accused if the judge submitted a relevant request and cases concerning crimes of a very complicated character or of special public importance, over which the Military Chamber is entitled to have jurisdiction if an accused has submitted a request.

4. The Military Chamber shall consider cases concerning complaints and appeals against decisions, convictions, definitions and judgments of the District (Fleet) Courts-Martial which were adopted by them in first instance and have not entered into force.

5. The Military Chamber shall consider cases concerning complaints and

appeals against decisions, convictions, definitions and judgments of courts-martial which have entered into force.

6. The Military Chamber shall consider cases concerning newly appeared circumstances in relation to decisions and judgments of the Military Chamber, which entered into force.

Article 10.   The Military Chamber

1. The Military Chamber shall act within the structure of the Supreme Court of the Russian Federation and shall be the direct higher court to District (Fleet) Courts-Martial.

2. The Military Chamber shall comprise the Chairman, Deputy Chairman, Chairmen of court staffs and other judges of the Supreme Court of the Russian Federation (hereinafter referred to as judges of the Military Chamber).

3. Military staffs may be formed in the Military Chamber.

4. The Military Chamber shall consider cases over which military courts have jurisdiction, composed of the following staff:

(1) in the first instance, civil and administrative cases shall be considered by a single judge or by the Chamber consisting of three judges, and criminal cases shall be considered by the Chamber consisting of three judges, or by a judge and the jury, or by the Chamber consisting of a judge and people's assessors;

(2) cases concerning complaints and appeals against decisions, convictions, definitions and judgments of District (Fleet) Courts-Martial which were adopted by them in the first instance and have not entered into force shall be considered by the Chamber consisting of three judges;

(3) cases concerning complaints and appeals against decisions, convictions, definitions and judgments of courts-martial which have entered into force shall be considered by the Chamber consisting of three judges.

5. The Military Chamber shall issue Information Report of Courts-Martial where the following is printed: decisions of courts-martial on civil and criminal cases, reviews on court practice, analytical materials, statistics on the work of courts-martial, and other materials.

Article 11.   Chairman of the Military Chamber of the Supreme Court of the Russian Federation

1. The Chairman of the Military Chamber of the Supreme Court of the Russian Federation (hereinafter referred to as the Chairman of the Military Chamber) is the Deputy Chairman of the Supreme Court of the Russian Federation and is appointed to this position by the Federation Council of the Federal Assembly of the Russian Federation after nomination by the President of the Russian Federation based on the nomination made by the Chairman of the Supreme Court of the Russian Federation and conclusions drawn by the Qualification Chamber of Judges of the Supreme Court of the Russian Federation.

2. The Chairman of the Military Chamber shall:

(1) submit protests to the Presidium of the Supreme Court of the Russian Federation against decisions, convictions, definitions and judgments of the

Military Chamber that have entered into force;

(2) submit protests to the Military Chamber and presidiums of District (Fleet) Courts-Martial against decisions, convictions, definitions and judgments of courts-martial that have entered into force;

(3) be entitled to participate in review of cases by the Military Chamber and act as Chairman in court hearings;

(4) organize activity of the Military Chamber;

(5) decide, if necessary, whether to transfer the case from one court staff to another;

(6) control the work of the staff of the Military Chamber that is a structural unit of the staff of the Supreme Court of the Russian Federation (hereinafter referred to as the staff of the Military Chamber) and appoint to positions and relieve the personnel of the Military Chamber of their posts;

(7) have other powers envisaged by federal law and perform duties that were entrusted by the Chairman of the Supreme Court of the Russian Federation.

Article 12.   Deputy Chairman of the Military Chamber, Chairman of the court staff

1. The Deputy Chairman of the Military Chamber shall:

(1) be entitled to participate in review of cases by the Military Chamber and act as a Chairman in court hearings;

(2) have powers of the Chairman of the Military Chamber while the latter is absent, excluding powers to submit protests;

(3) perform other duties entrusted by the Chairman of the Supreme Court of the Russian Federation and by the Chairman of the Military Chamber.

2. The Chairman of the court staff shall:

(1) organize the work of the court staff;

(2) participate in review of cases by the court staff and act as Chairman in court hearings of the court staff;

(3) control the work of personnel of the court staff;

(4) perform duties entrusted by the Chairman of the Military Chamber.

Article 13.   District (Fleet) Court-Martial

1. The District (Fleet) Court-Martial shall act in the territory of one or several bodies of the Russian Federation, on which military units and institutions of the Armed Forces of the Russian Federation, of other troops, military formations and agencies are located.

2. The District (Fleet) Court-Martial shall comprise Chairman, Deputy Chairman and other judges. The position of First Deputy Chairman may be included in the District (Fleet) Court-Martial.

3. The presidium shall be formed in the District (Fleet) Court-Martial, and Military Chambers and/or court staffs may be formed there.

Article 14.   Jurisdiction of the District (Fleet) Court-Martial

1. Within the limits determined by this Federal Constitutional Law, the District (Fleet) Court-Martial shall consider in the first instance civil cases concerning state secrets and cases about crimes for which punishment may be imposed in the form of imprisonment for a period of more than 15 years, life imprisonment or capital punishment.

2. Within the limits determined by this Federal Constitutional Law, the District (Fleet) Court-Martial shall consider cases concerning complaints and appeals against decisions, convictions, definitions and judgments of garrison courts martial that were adopted by them in the first instance and have not entered into force.

3. Within the limits determined by this Federal Constitutional Law, the District (Fleet) Court-Martial shall consider cases concerning complaints and appeals against decisions, convictions, definitions and judgments of garrison courts martial that have entered into force and judgments that were adopted by District (Fleet) Court-Martial in the second instance.

4. The District (Fleet) Court-Martial shall consider cases concerning newly appeared circumstances in relation to decisions and judgments of the District (Fleet) Court-Martial which entered into force.

Article 15.   Personnel of the District (Fleet) Court-Martial while administering justice

1. The District (Fleet) Court-Martial in the first instance shall consider cases which fall within its jurisdiction according to this Federal Constitutional Law, composed of the following staff:

(1) civil and administrative cases shall be considered by a single judge or by the Chamber composed of three judges;

(2) criminal cases shall be considered by the Chamber composed of three judges, or a judge and the jury, or by the Chamber composed of a judge and people's assessors.

2. The District (Fleet) Court-Martial shall consider cases concerning complaints and appeals against decisions, convictions, definitions and judgments of garrison courts martial that were adopted by them in the first instance and have not yet entered into force, and concerning complaints and appeals against decisions of garrison courts martial on detention, custody, limitations of rights to the confidentiality of correspondence, telephone and other communications, post, telegraph and other messages, on inviolability of the home, on action (or inaction) of officials making an inquiry, of investigator, prosecutor and on decisions adopted by them, — by the Chamber composed of three judges.

3. The District (Fleet) Court-Martial shall consider at the meetings of the Presidium cases concerning appeals against decisions, convictions, definitions and judgments of garrison courts martial that entered into force, as well as against decisions and judgments that were adopted by the District (Fleet) Court-Martial in the second instance.

Article 16.   Presidium of the District (Fleet) Court-Martial

1. The Presidium of the District (Fleet) Court-Martial shall act as composed by the Chairman, Deputy Chairman — Chairmen of Court Chambers and court staffs.

2. The Presidium of the District (Fleet) Court-Martial shall:

(1) consider civil, administrative and criminal cases concerning appeals against decisions, convictions, definitions and judgments of garrison courts martial that entered into force, as well as against decisions and judgments that were adopted by the District (Fleet) Court-Martial in the second instance;

(2) consider questions of organization of work and coordinate the work of Court Chambers and court staffs;

(3) appoint Chairmen of Court Chambers and Court staffs upon nomination of the Chairman of the Court;

(4) determine the number of Court Chambers and Court staffs upon nomination of the Chairman of the Court;

(5) consider questions of organization of work of the Court staff, approve the structure and schedule of the court personnel, number of staff and regulations on the court staff upon nomination by the Chairman of the Court.

Article 17. Order of Work of the Presidium of the District (Fleet) Court-Martial

1. Meetings of the District (Fleet) Court-Martial shall be held not less than once per month on the initiative of the Chairman of the Court.

2. The meeting of the Presidium of the District (Fleet) Court-Martial shall have quorum if more than half members are present.

3. The judgments of the District (Fleet) Court-Martial shall be adopted by the majority of votes of the members who are present at the meeting.

Article 18. Court Chambers and Court Staffs of the District (Fleet) Court-Martial

The Court Chambers and Court Staffs of the District (Fleet) Court-Martial shall consider:

(1) in first instance cases that fall under the jurisdiction of the District (Fleet) Court-Martial according to this Federal Constitutional Law;

(2) cases about complaints and appeals against decisions, convictions, definitions and judgments of garrison courts martial that were adopted by them in the first instance and that have not entered into force;

(3) cases on newly appeared circumstances related to decisions, convictions, definitions and judgments that were adopted by the relevant Court Chamber, Court Staff and that entered into force.

Article 19. Chairman of the District (Fleet) Court-Martial

1. The Chairman of the District (Fleet) Court-Martial shall be appointed to this position by the President of the Russian Federation upon the nomination of the Chairman of the Supreme Court of the Russian Federation based on the

conclusions of the Supreme Qualification Chamber of Judges of the Supreme Court of the Russian Federation.

2. The Chairman of the District (Fleet) Court-Martial shall:

(1) submit protests against decisions, convictions, definitions and judgments of the relevant garrison and District (Fleet) Courts Martial that have entered into force;

(2) be entitled to participate in examination of cases by a District (Fleet) Court-Martial and act as Chairman in court hearings;

(3) organize court activities;

(4) convene meetings of the Presidium of the Court and submit to it cases that shall be examined and preside at the meetings of the Presidium;

(5) delegate duties to the Deputy Chairmen of the Court;

(6) decide, if necessary, whether to transfer cases from one court Chamber or Court staff to another Court Chamber or Court staff, and also decide questions concerning the appointment of a Court Chamber or Court staff to examine cases in another Court Chamber or Court staff;

(7) control the work of the Administrator and court personnel, appoint to a post and relieve court personnel of their posts if they do not perform military service;

(8) represent the Court in state agencies, public organizations and bodies of self government;

(9) have other powers envisaged by federal law.

Article 20. **Deputy Chairman of the District (Fleet) Court-Martial, Deputy Chairman — Chairman of the Court Chamber or Court staff of the District (Fleet) Court-Martial, Chairman of the Court staff of the District (Fleet) Court-Martial**

1. The Deputy Chairman of the District (Fleet) Court-Martial shall be appointed to this post by the President of the Russian Federation upon the nomination of the Chairman of the Supreme Court of the Russian Federation based on the conclusions of the Supreme Qualification Chamber of Judges of the Russian Federation.

The Deputy Chairman of the District (Fleet) Court-Martial, Deputy Chairman — Chairman of the Court Chamber or Court staff of the District (Fleet) Court-Martial, Chairman of the Court staff of the District (Fleet) Court-Martial shall:

(1) be entitled to participate in the review of cases by the relevant Court Chamber or Court Staff and preside at court hearings;

(2) organize the work of the relevant Court Chamber or Court staff;

(3) control the work of personnel of the relevant Court Chamber or Court staff;

(4) have other powers envisaged by federal law and perform duties that were entrusted by the Chairman of the Court.

3. The Deputy Chairman of the District (Fleet) Court-Martial shall have powers of the Chairman of the District (Fleet) Court-Martial while the latter is

absent, excluding the powers to submit protests, and shall perform other duties at the Chairman's request.

4. The Deputy Chairman of the District (Fleet) Court-Martial shall:

(1) be entitled to participate in the review of cases by the Court Staff and preside at court hearings;

(2) organize the work of the Court staff;

(3) control the work of personnel of the Court staff;

(4) have other powers envisaged by federal law and perform duties that were entrusted by the Chairman of the Court and/or the Chairman of the relevant Court Chamber.

Article 21.   Garrison Court-Martial

1. The Garrison Court-Martial shall operate in the territory on which one or more military garrisons are located.

2. The Garrison Court-Martial shall be composed of the Chairman, Deputy Chairmen and other judges.

Article 22.   Jurisdiction of the Garrison Court-Martial

1. Within the scope envisaged by this Federal Constitutional Law, the Garrison Court-Martial shall consider in the first instance civil, administrative and criminal cases that are not assigned by this Federal Constitutional Law to the jurisdiction of the Military Chamber or the District (Fleet) Court-Martial.

The Garrison Court-Martial shall consider cases on newly appeared circumstances related to decisions, convictions, definitions and judgments that were adopted by the Garrison Court-Martial and that entered into force.

3. The Garrison Court-Martial shall make decisions on detention, custody, limitations of rights to the confidentiality of correspondence, telephone and other communications, post, telegraph and other messages and on inviolability of the home.

4. The Garrison Court-Martial shall consider complaints and appeals against action (or inaction) of officials making an inquiry, of investigator, prosecutor and on decisions adopted by them in the order and cases that are determined by the Federal Criminal Procedure Law.

Article 23.   Staff of the Garrison Court-Martial while administering justice

1. The Garrison Court-Martial shall consider cases in the first instance by the following staff:

(1) civil and administrative cases shall be considered by a single judge or by a Chamber composed of a judge and people's assessors if any of the parties submits a relevant request;

(2) criminal cases shall be considered by a single judge or by a Chamber composed of a judge and people's assessors.

2. A judge of a Garrison Court-Martial shall solely make decisions on detention, custody, limitations of rights to the confidentiality of correspondence, telephone

and other communications, post, telegraph and other messages, on inviolability of the home, and shall consider complaints and appeals against action (inaction) of officials making an inquiry, of investigator, prosecutor and on decisions adopted by them in the order and cases that are determined by the Federal Criminal Procedure Law.

Article 24. Chairman of the Garrison Court-Martial

1. The Chairman of the Garrison Court-Martial shall be appointed to this post by the President of the Russian Federation upon the nomination of the Chairman of the Supreme Court of the Russian Federation based on the conclusions of the Supreme Qualification Chamber of Judges of the Russian Federation.

2. The Chairman of the Garrison Court-Martial shall:

(1) be entitled to participate in the review of cases by the Garrison Court-Martial and preside at court hearings;

(2) organize the work of the court;

(3) delegate duties to judges;

(4) control the work of the Administrator and personnel of the court, appoint to posts and relieve personnel of the Court Staff of their posts if they do not perform military service and adopt regulations on the Court Staff;

(5) represent the Court in state agencies, public organizations and bodies of self government.

Article 25. Deputy Chairman of the Garrison Court-Martial

1. The Deputy Chairman of the Garrison Court-Martial shall be appointed to this post by the President of the Russian Federation upon the nomination of the Chairman of the Supreme Court of the Russian Federation based on the conclusions of the Supreme Qualification Chamber of Judges of the Russian Federation.

2. Along with performing duties of the judge, the Deputy Chairman of the Garrison Court-Martial shall act as Chairman of the Garrison Court-Martial while the latter is absent and shall perform other duties at the Chairman's request.

CHAPTER III. STATUS OF COURTS-MARTIAL JUDGES

Article 26. Peculiarities of Status of Judges of Courts-Martial and the Military Chamber

1. The status of judges of courts-martial and the Military Chamber shall be determined according to the Constitution of the Russian Federation, the Federal Constitutional Law on the Court System of the Russian Federation, the Law of the Russian Federation on the Status of Judges in the Russian Federation, this Federal Constitutional Law, Federal Constitutional laws, and federal laws.

2. Appointment of a court-martial judge to another post in the same court or transfer of the judge to another court-martial shall be made with the consent of the judge, excluding cases of transfer of the judge to a court-martial that is situated outside the territory of the Russian Federation or that is operating in an

area where a state of emergency has been declared.

3. Judges of courts-martial who are fit for military service, taking into account their health conditions, cannot be discharged from military service without their consent till they reach the age limit for military service that is envisaged by federal laws. The term of military service for judges of courts-martial who reach the age limit for being in the relevant military rank may be prolonged to 10 years by the Chairman of the Supreme Court of the Russian Federation on the recommendation of the Qualification Chamber of Judges of Courts-Martial, but not past age 65.

Article 27.   Requirements that Candidates for the Position of Court-Martial Judge shall Meet

A court-martial judge shall be a citizen of the Russian Federation who has reached the age of 25 years, who has higher law education, not less than five years experience in law, who has not committed any misconduct, and who has passed a qualification exam and obtained recommendation of the Qualification Chamber of Judges of Courts-Martial and who has an officer rank and has concluded the Contract on Military Service.

Article 28.   Status of the Jury and People's Assessors of Courts-Martial and the Military Chamber

The status of the jury and people's assessors of courts-martial and the Military Chamber and the order of invitation of citizens of the Russian Federation to administer justice as the jury and people's assessors shall be determined by Federal Constitutional Laws and federal laws.

Article 29.   Peculiarities of Material Security of Judges of Courts-Martial and the Military Chamber

1. A money allowance shall be paid to judges of courts-martial and the Military Chamber on the grounds and in the amounts determined for judges by federal law. Judges of courts-martial and the Military Chamber shall be entitled to receive other payments that are provided for judges by federal law.

2. Judges of courts-martial and the Military Chamber shall also be paid salaries according to their military ranks on the grounds and in the amounts determined for military persons by federal law.

3. Judges of courts-martial and the Military Chamber shall have a choice whether to receive either long service bonus on the grounds and in the amount defined for judges by federal law, or long service interest payment on the grounds and in the amount defined for military persons by relevant legal regulation acts.

4. Awarding a premium to judges of courts-martial and the Military Chamber and granting material aid to them shall be made on the grounds and in the amount that are envisaged for judges by federal law.

5. In case of honorable resignation (discharge) of judges of courts-martial and the Military Chamber and at the same time of discharge from military service, the above mentioned judges shall be entitled to receive at their choice either a

lump sum allowance upon their discharge from military service, that is envisaged for military persons by federal law, or gratuity that is envisaged by the Law of the Russian Federation on the Status of Judges in the Russian Federation. Judges of courts-martial and the Military Chamber who have received a gratuity for the period of service as a judge and who have remained in military service, shall not be entitled to receive a lump sum allowance for the above mentioned period upon their discharge from military service.

6. Judges of courts-martial and the Military Chamber who have the right to receive a monthly life allowance in full amount or long service military pensions and who continue to work as Judges shall be entitled to receive at their choice either a monthly bonus to money allowance which is calculated in percentage from the monthly life allowance that might be awarded to them at the time of retirement or a percentage bonus of the pension that might be awarded to them for long military service.

Article 30. Living Allowance and Pension of Judges of Courts-Martial and the Military Chamber

1. In case of honorable resignation (discharge) of judges of courts-martial and the Military Chamber and at the same time of discharge from military service, the above mentioned judges shall be entitled to receive at their choice either the tax free monthly living allowance, that is envisaged for judges by federal law, or the pension that is envisaged for military persons, or the pension that is envisaged for Judges of courts-martial and the Military Chamber shall be entitled to the pension that is envisaged for military personnel and calculated on the basis of their salary, taking into account their position. The increase in pension, if it is reviewed later in cases envisaged by federal law, shall be calculated taking into account the above-mentioned salary.

2. The period of service (including the period before this Federal Constitutional Law entered into force) in the position of court-martial judge located outside the territory of the Russian Federation and in regions and areas of the Russian Federation where according to the legislation of the Russian Federation military personnel have a right to special calculation of long military service term, shall be taken into consideration for the calculation of long service of judges of courts-martial in the position of judges in the order determined for calculation of long military service in the relevant Military Court, region and area.

Article 31. Peculiarities of Social Security of Judges of Courts-Martial and the Military Chamber, and members of their family

1. Judges of courts-martial and the Military Chamber and members of their families and their property are under special protection of the State. The Interior services and the command of military units in the place of dislocation of a court-martial shall take necessary measures to provide security to judges of courts-martial and the Military Chamber, members of their families and safety of their property according to the federal law on "State Security of Judges, Officials of Law Enforcement Agencies and Inspections."

2. If a court-martial judge or judge of the Military Chamber (including retired judges) dies not because of the judge's service duties, disabled members of the

judge's family who were the judge's dependents shall be entitled, at the choice of agencies responsible for pensions of judges and military personnel, to receive the pension which might be awarded to a court-martial judge or to a judge of the Military Chamber on the grounds determined by this Federal Constitutional Law, the Law of the Russian Federation on "Pensions to individuals who performed military service, service in the agencies of the Interior, institutions and agencies of criminal executive system and to members of their families" or the Law of the Russian Federation on "the Status of Judges of the Russian Federation."

3. Judges of courts-martial and the Military Chamber shall be granted at their request main annual paid leaves and additional leaves in the order envisaged by federal law either for judges or for military personnel.

4. Housing shall be provided to judges of courts-martial and the Military Chamber in out of turn order by the relevant bodies of the Armed Forces of the Russian Federation, other troops, military formations and agencies with the following compensation of their expenses from the funds of the federal budget or shall be bought with the money of the federal budget allocated for these aims according to the requirements defined in the Law of the Russian Federation "On the Status of Judges in the Russian Federation," not later than within six months since the judge was entrusted with powers.

5. Living quarters that are occupied by judges of courts-martial and the Military Chamber in houses of state or municipal dwelling funds and in case it is vacated, shall be granted to other court-martial judges and to personnel of the Court staff who need their living conditions to be improved in accordance with the requirements defined by federal law.

6. Medical service for judges of courts-martial (including retired judges) and members of their families, including provision of medicine and facilities in sanatoria and health resorts, shall be in accordance with standards and in the order that are determined for judges by federal law. The above-mentioned service, provision and facilities of judges of courts-martial shall be supplied by relevant agencies of the Armed Forces of the Russian Federation, other troops, military formations and bodies and, as far as judges of the Military Chamber are concerned, in the order prescribed for judges of the Supreme Court of the Russian Federation.

7. Judges of courts-martial, the Military Chamber and members of their families shall have the right to use at their discretion privileges and compensations that are envisaged by federal law either for judges and members of their family or for military personnel and members of their families.

CHAPTER IV.   FINANCING AND PROVISION FOR THE ACTIVITIES OF COURTS-MARTIAL AND THE MILITARY CHAMBER

Article 32.   Financing and Provision for Courts-Martial and the Military Chamber

1. Courts-martial and the Military Chamber shall be financed with the funds of the Federal budget by the Court Department attached to the Supreme Court of the Russian Federation (hereinafter referred to as the Court Department) and

by the Supreme Court of the Russian Federation respectively in accordance with the Federal Constitutional Law "On the Court System of the Russian Federation" and by this Federal Constitutional Law.

2. Provision of courts-martial, the Military Chamber and the relevant unit of the Court Department with transport, communication means, armament, service premises, maintenance, operation and security of such premises, and archives keeping shall be supplied by relevant agencies of the Armed Forces of the Russian Federation, other troops, military formations and other agencies the incurred expenses shall be paid by the Court Department and the Supreme Court of the Russian Federation respectively.

3. Organizational provision of the Military Chamber shall be supplied by the Staff of the Supreme Court of the Russian Federation, and as far as courts-martial are concerned, by the Court Department.

4. The order of financing and provision of courts-martial in wartime and in a state of emergency shall be determined by relevant Federal Constitutional Laws.

Article 33.   Staffs of the Court-Martial and the Military Chamber

1. The staffs of the court-martial and the Military Chamber shall provide for administration of justice by courts-martial and the Military Chamber respectively, summary of court practice, analysis of court statistics, systematization of legislation and performance of other functions of the court.

2. The staff of the court-martial and the staff of the Military Chamber shall be governed by heads of the relevant staffs. The operations of the staff of the court-martial and the staff of the Military Chamber shall be controlled by the Chairman of the Court-Martial and the Chairman of the Military Chamber respectively.

3. The structure and schedule of the staff of the court-martial and the number of personnel shall be determined within the limits of the funds that were allocated by the Presidium of the relevant court and, if the Presidium is not established, by the chairman of the relevant court. The structure and schedule of the staff of the Military Chamber and the number of personnel shall be determined within the limits of the funds that were allocated by the Chairman of the Supreme Court of the Russian Federation.

4. The following posts shall be envisaged in the staffs of courts-martial and the Military Chamber: Assistant Chairman of the Court, Assistant Judges, Heads of Departments, Deputy Heads of Departments, Counsellors, Consultants, Chief Specialists, Leading Specialists, Specialists of the 1st category, Specialists of the 2nd category and Specialists.

5. Personnel of the staffs of courts-martial and the Military Chamber shall be considered to be officials of the State. Military personnel may be attached to the staffs of courts-martial and the Military Chamber. The rights and duties of the above mentioned personnel and the order of their performing state service shall be determined by federal laws and other legal regulations on federal state service. These personnel shall be given class ranks and special ranks and military persons shall also be given military ranks.

6. Personnel of the staffs of courts-martial and the Military Chamber shall be

certified once every three years. The order of certification shall be defined by the Regulations on Attestation of Personnel of the Staffs of Federal Court of Common Jurisdiction and adopted by the Chairman of the Supreme Court of the Russian Federation. Certification of military personnel who are attached to the staffs of courts-martial and the Military Chamber shall be carried out in the order adopted in the Armed Forces of the Russian Federation.

7. Personnel of the staffs of courts-martial and the Military Chamber (including military persons) and members of their family shall be entitled to regulations on material allowance, measures of social protection and other legal and social guarantees that are defined by federal law for the personnel of staffs of federal courts of common jurisdiction and for the members of their family.

8. Salaries of personnel on the staffs of courts-martial and the Military Chamber from military personnel shall be determined in relation to salaries of corresponding personnel of the staffs of Federal Courts of common jurisdiction. The above mentioned personnel shall also be paid salaries for their military ranks and a percentage long service bonus on the grounds and in the amounts defined by federal law for military personnel.

9. Pensions of personnel of the staffs of courts-martial and the Military Chamber from military persons shall be paid in accordance with the Law of the Russian Federation on Pension allowance of individuals who performed military service, service in the Interior, institutions and agencies of criminal executive system and of their family members. Pensions shall be granted to the above-mentioned personnel, taking into account salaries that they had in their positions. In cases of the further review of the amount of pension as envisaged by federal law, the rise in pension shall be granted, taking into account the said salaries.

10. The regulations for the staff of the Military Chamber shall be adopted by the Chairman of the Military Chamber.

Article 34.   Administrator of the Court-Martial

1. The Administrator of the court-martial shall:

(1) take measures on organizational provision of the court;

(2) cooperate with state agencies, public associations, bodies of local self government, their officials and other personnel on the question of provision of the court;

(3) take measures on providing judges of courts-martial and personnel of the staff of the court-martial with necessary material and life conditions, medical service and facilities of sanatoria and health resorts;

(4) supply judges of the court-martial and personnel of the staff of the court-martial with law literature, manuals and reference and information materials;

(5) supply information and legal provision to courts-martial, organize court statistics, record-keeping and work of archives;

(6) organize the guard of the building, premises and other property of the court-martial in non-working time, provide for transportation of the court-martial, communications means and work of household services;

(7) organize construction of premises, as well as reconstruction and technical equipment of buildings and premises of the court-martial;

(8) make up draft estimates of expenses of the court-martial that shall be adopted by the Chairman of the court-martial, and submit it to a relevant unit of the Court Department;

(9) take other measures on provision of the court-martial;

(10) fulfill orders and directions of the Chairman of the court-martial that are connected with provision of the court-martial.

2. The Administrator of the court-martial shall perform his/her duties under control of the chairman of the relevant court and under direction of the corresponding unit of the Court Department.

3. The Administrator of the court-martial shall be appointed and relieved by the head of the relevant unit of the Court Department on nomination by the Chairman of the relevant court-martial.

Article 35. Peculiarities of Staffing of Courts-Martial, the Military Chamber and the Court Department

1. To posts of judges of courts-martial, the Military Chamber and envisaged by schedule state positions of personnel of the staffs of courts-martial, the Military Chamber and the Court Department, military personnel who are attached to courts-martial, the Supreme Court of the Russian Federation and the Court Department shall be appointed in the order defined by the Federal Law on Military Duty and Military Service, taking into account the provisions of this Federal Constitutional Law. Military persons shall be attached upon the nomination of the Chairman of the Supreme Court of the Russian Federation.

2. Limits on the attachment of military persons to courts-martial, the Supreme Court of the Russian Federation, and the Court Department shall be established from the number of the Armed Forces of the Russian Federation, other troops, military formations and agencies in proportion to the number of the Armed Forces of the Russian Federation, other troops, military formations and agencies respectively, and shall be adopted by the President of the Russian Federation upon the presentation of the Chairman of the Supreme Court of the Russian Federation.

3. Judges of courts-martial and the Military Chamber, personnel of the staffs of courts-martial, the Military Chamber and the Court Department from the number of military persons shall be attached to courts-martial, the Supreme Court of the Russian Federation and the Court Department for the period of holding the following position.

4. The Contract on Military Service executed by the judge of the court-martial and the judges of the Military Chamber before nomination to a judicial position shall be suspended from the moment the decision on appointment of the judge to a post was adopted by the Federation Council of the Federal Assembly of the Russian Federation or by the President of the Russian Federation. Judges of courts-martial and the Military Chamber shall retain the status of military persons who perform military service in accordance with the Contract. In case the powers of judges of courts-martial and the Military Chamber cease according

to the Law of the Russian Federation on the Status of Judges in the Russian Federation, the Contract on Military Service shall be valid again as defined by the Federal Law on Military Duties and Military Service.

5. The list of positions of judges of courts-martial and the Military Chamber and military ranks corresponding to these positions shall be determined by this Federal Constitutional Law.

6. Military persons attached to the Court Department who are providing for the operation of courts-martial shall be appointed to state posts that are determined for the Court Department.

7. The list of positions of personnel of the staffs of courts-martial, the Military Chamber and the Court Department that are to be filled by military personnel, and of military ranks corresponding to these positions shall be adopted by the Chairman of the Supreme Court of the Russian Federation. The positions of judges of courts-martial and the Military Chamber and the positions of personnel of the staffs of courts-martial, the Military Chamber and the Court Department that are to be filled by military personnel shall be included in the relevant list of positions.

Article 36.   Order of Performing Military Service in Courts-Martial and the Military Chamber

1. Judges of courts-martial and the Military Chamber, personnel of the staffs of courts-martial, the Military Chamber and the Court Department from the number of military personnel shall perform military service in accordance with the Federal Law on Military Duties and Military Service, taking into account provisions of this Federal Constitutional Law.

2. Judges of courts-martial and the Military Chamber shall be given higher military ranks in the order envisaged by the Federal Law on Military Duties and Military Service on the nomination of the Chairman of the Supreme Court of the Russian Federation, other military ranks — upon the nomination of Chairmen of District (Fleet) Courts-Martial.

3. Military ranks in the order envisaged by the Federal Law on Military Duties and Military Service shall be given to personnel of courts-martial, the Military Chamber and the Court Department from the number of military personnel upon the nomination of:

(1) the Chairman of the Military Chamber — for personnel of the staff of the Military Chamber;

(2) the Chairman of the District (Fleet) Court-Martial — for personnel of the staffs of a relevant District (Fleet) Court-Martial and Garrison Court-Martial;

(3) Director General of the Court Department — for personnel of the Court Department.

4. Appointment to the position and dismissal from the position, as well as transfer or removal to another position of personnel of the staffs of courts-martial from the number of military persons shall be made by the head of the relevant subdivision of the Court Department, and the personnel of the staff of the Military Chamber — by the Chairman of the Military Chamber.

5. Personnel of the staffs of courts-martial, the Military Chamber and the Court Department from the number of military persons shall be paid a lump sum allowance upon the discharge from military service and all additional money allowances that are defined for military persons by federal law. In this case the amount of money allowances shall be calculated taking into account salaries of personnel of the staffs of the courts-martial, the Military Chamber and the Court Department from the number of military persons.

6. Clothing, food and other provision of judges of courts-martial and the Military Chamber, as well as of personnel of the staffs of courts-martial, the Military Chamber and the Court Department from the number of military personnel shall be supplied on the basis and in the amounts that are defined for military personnel by federal law.

7. Medical service, facilities of sanatoria and health resorts, dwelling provision, clothing, food and other provision, compulsory state insurance of judges of courts-martial, as well as personnel of the staffs of the courts-martial, the Military Chamber and the Court Department from the number of military personnel, granting of other privileges and compensations, that are envisaged for military personnel by federal law, shall be provided by the relevant bodies of the Armed Forces of the Russian Federation, other troops, military formations and agencies at the expense of the Supreme Court of the Russian Federation and the Court Department respectively.

8. Personnel of the staffs of the courts-martial, the Military Chamber and the Court Department from the number of military persons and members of their family shall have the right at their discretion to use privileges and compensations, that are envisaged by federal law either for personnel of the staffs of Federal Courts of common jurisdiction and the members of their family, or for military personnel and members of their family.

9. Military registration of judges of courts-martial and personnel of the staffs of courts-martial who were discharged from military service and safekeeping of their personal records shall be carried out by the relevant Military Commissariats in the order, envisaged by federal law.

Article 37. Premises and Other Property of Courts-Martial

1. Courts-martial shall be located in premises which have exteriors and interiors corresponding to the constitutional status of the judicial power in the Russian Federation.

2. To administer justice, a court-martial judge shall be granted premises that meet sanitary and hygienic standards and other standards that are defined.

3. Premises, buildings and movable property shall be used by courts-martial solely for the purpose of administering justice or organizational provision of the court operation and shall be considered to be federal property. The above mentioned property cannot be seized.

4. Courts-martial shall be free of rent and other payments for the use of land that is allocated for construction of buildings and premises which are in possession of courts-martial; courts-martial shall be free of communal and other payments for the maintenance of these buildings and premises.

Article 38.   Guarding and Escorting of Individuals Held in Custody

1. In courts-martial, guarding of individuals held in disciplinary military units, held in custody in guardroom and their escorting shall be carried out by military units or the military commandant's office of the garrison respectively.

2. Escorting of individuals who are located in the place of detention, prisons and reformatory to a place where the court-martial examines cases shall be carried out by the authorized federal bodies of executive power.

CHAPTER V.   CLOSING AND TRANSITIONAL PROVISIONS [OMITTED]

Positions of Judges of Courts-Martial and the Military Chamber of the Supreme Court of the Russian Federation and Corresponding Military Ranks

No.	Position	Military Rank
1.	Chairman of the Military Chamber of the Supreme Court of the Russian Federation	Colonel General of Justice
2.	Deputy Chairman of the Military Chamber of the Supreme Court of the Russian Federation, Chairman of the Staff of the Military Chamber of the Supreme Court of the Russian Federation; Chairman of Moscow District Court-Martial	Lieutenant General of Justice
3.	Judge of the Military Chamber of the Supreme Court of the Russian Federation; Chairman of District (Fleet) Court-Martial; Deputy Chairman of Moscow District Court-Martial; Chairman of Moscow Garrison Court-Martial	Major Colonel of Justice
4.	Deputy Chairman and Judge of District (Fleet) Court-Martial; Chairman of Garrison Court-Martial; Deputy Chairman of Moscow Garrison Court-Martial	Colonel of Justice
5.	Deputy Chairman and Judge of Garrison Court-Martial	Lieutenant Colonel of Justice